THE AGE OF GLOBAL GIVING

Endorsements

One of the key arenas in which Satan has a foothold is in the relationship between donors and the ministries they support. Distrust, pride, insecurity, imperfect information, fear, and miscommunication combine to give Satan the opportunity to create division within the body of Christ and to slow the advancement of the kingdom. In this important book, Gilles Gravelle argues that ministries need to repent of a "pay, pray, and get out of the way" attitude towards their donors. In the place of this, he argues for a more biblical model in which donors and ministries see each other as full partners in ministry, seeking to humbly respect the full range of each other's gifts and stewardship responsibilities. This is an important work addressing a very timely issue.

Brian Fikkert
co-author of *When Helping Hurts: How to Alleviate Poverty Without Hurting the Poor . . . and Yourself*

Gilles Gravelle makes the case for fully enfranchising an important and often missing partner in global missions—the major donor. For too long, donors with wealth and wisdom have been sidelined by ministries—thanked for their gifts and fed reports at a safe distance from "the real work." There's a new, activist generation of donors with more to give than a check. Gilles shows that ministries can successfully include the perspectives, faith, and financial investment of major donors and foundations, benefiting from seasoned business insights, advocacy, and passionate commitment to seeing changed lives. The dividing wall of separation between donors and those leading ministry has been breached, and Gilles persuasively explains why it ought to come down altogether.

Paul Edwards
vice president for Strategic Thinking, Wycliffe USA

Giving is emerging as a key theme in the global Christian community. Scholars such as Ron Sider, Tom Sine, Jonathan Bonk, Vinay Samuel, Brian Fikkert, Glenn Schwartz, and Mary Lederleitner have written on different issues around poverty, wealth, income inequality, a Christian approach to money, self-reliance, and mobilizing giving. In the US ministries such as Crown Financial Ministries, the National Christian Foundation, Generous Church, and Generous Giving facilitate thinking and engagement around giving related issues. One of the most important and most sensitive issues that have to be addressed is the relationship between donors and ministries. In a globalized and increasingly interdependent Christian community, Gilles Gravelle will definitely stimulate thinking and discussion around what Rob Martin of the First Fruit Institute calls "The Communion of Givers and Receivers." That was the impact on me when I read the manuscript!

Sas Conradie, DD
coordinator of the Lausanne Movement/World Evangelical
Alliance Global Generosity Network

Everyone engaged in the giving or receiving of financial resources for kingdom purposes must read *The Age of Global Giving*. Here Gilles Gravelle succinctly presents the historic positions, persistent errors, and enormous potentials of effectual relationships between major donors and ministry implementers. The case Gilles builds for "relationships first" forms the foundation for trust and accountability that is essential in continuing and accelerating beyond the status quo in missions that has been carried forward from the twentieth century. Here is a guide that helps leaders with kingdom hearts expand their impact and influence through partnerships overshadowed by the cross of Jesus Christ.

Joe Class
chairman of the board, Sequoia Global Resources

Gilles Gravelle is right on target as to the heart of the emerging generation and its philanthropy. Breaking down the walls between organization and philanthropist is critical to engagement. Gilles gives practical steps to implement to help any agency wanting to grow their engagement with major financial partners. It all comes together like hand in glove when financial partners are involved at the strategic level with your organization.

John Lind
chief development officer, Frontiers USA

THE AGE OF GLOBAL GIVING

A practical guide for the donors and
funding recipients of our time

GILLES GRAVELLE

WILLIAM CAREY
LIBRARY

*The Age of Global Giving: A Practical Guide for the
Donors and Recipients of Our Time*

Copyright © 2014 Gilles Gravelle

Published by William Carey Library
1605 E. Elizabeth St.
Pasadena, CA 91104 | www.missionbooks.org

Mel Hughes, editor
Mel Hughes, copyeditor
Josie Leung, graphic design

William Carey Library is a ministry of the
U.S. Center for World Mission
Pasadena, CA | www.uscwm.org

Printed in the United States of America

18 17 16 15 14   5 4 3 2 1 BP

Library of Congress Cataloging-in-Publication Data

Gravelle, Gilles.
  The age of global giving : a practical guide for the donors and funding recipients of our
time / Gilles Gravelle.
     pages cm
  Includes bibliographical references and index.
  ISBN 978-0-87808-539-2 -- ISBN 0-87808-539-4 1. Missions--Finance. 2. Christian
giving. 3. Finance, Personal--Religious aspects--Christianity. I. Title.
  BV2081.G73 2014

  266.0068'1--dc23

                              2014016556

Stewardship—which requires possessions and includes giving—
is the true spirit of discipline in relation to wealth.
Dallas Willard, *The Spirit of the Disciplines*

CONTENTS

LIST OF FIGURES

FOREWORD

I was at a meeting recently with researchers from several seminaries across North America. In one of the sessions Daniel Aleshire, Executive Director of the Association of Theological Schools, spoke on the topic "Financing the Call to Serve: Some Reflections on Ministry, Money and Theological Education." In his talk he said there might be more agreement about the Holy Trinity than there is agreement about what people in ministry should earn.

As I have been reflecting upon his comments, I believe a similar statement applies to our topic at hand. There might be more agreement about the theological mysteries of the Trinity than there is about how to fund global mission. Gilles Gravelle's book is deeply controversial in some missiological sectors. He believes strongly that the method of funding missions he proposes is preferable to other methods. He has developed this conviction over time and in the following pages he will argue his point passionately.

The reason I agreed to write a foreword to this text is not because I personally agree with all of his statements. For instance, Gilles quotes a line from Jim Plueddemann's book *Leading Across Cultures* that states weaknesses in mission projects in Africa are frequently the result of poor planning. However, the thesis of Jim's book is to help all leaders realize they have biases, and there is no "one right way" to lead in missions. He provides numerous illustrations about the validity of many African ways of leading. Gilles argues against the use of short-term missions trips, yet Jenny Collins and others have shown that if best practices are followed they can be a blessing in global mission, and I have seen this to be the case. Gilles also argues against funding and sending missionaries from countries like the United States. However, one of the reasons Gilles is such a seasoned and skilled missiologist is because of the perspective and experience he gained through years serving abroad as a missionary.

If I find myself at times disagreeing with Gilles' book, why agree to write a foreword for it? I willingly agreed to write the foreword because in this era of global mission I think it is essential for most leaders in ministry to understand the changing dynamic that Gilles addresses. Many ministries that once relied on small gifts from many donors are now more intentionally pursuing larger financial contributions. Without this "major donor" strategy as a significant piece of their funding model, many mission organizations are finding it difficult to weather financial challenges in the twenty-first century.

However, as Gilles aptly explains, the expectation of many wealthier funders has changed significantly in the recent past. As he so rightly argues, they too are part of the body of Christ, and their contribution and voice need to be heard. They are not ATM machines called to dole out funding while remaining silent. Many are godly men and women who are also called by God to use their resources in the kingdom. They are not second-class citizens in the body of Christ, inferior due to a false dualistic view that some *do* ministry whiles others just *fund* ministry. Many of these people now want to be integrally involved in *doing,* and when this tension is navigated well, there can be a better outcome for everyone.

Gilles builds the validity of this model primarily on a couple of significant passages of Scripture. It can be argued that other passages validate additional funding models. In writing the foreword to this text I am not arguing that other models be discarded or sidelined. Rather, I believe Gilles' book makes a significant contribution to the ever deepening and widening dialogue surrounding the funding of global mission. As such, I believe it is wholly worth your money and time to read and thoughtfully reflect upon his perspective. I will be strongly recommending it to both mission practitioners and students alike in the coming months and years.

Mary Lederleitner, PhD
author of *Cross-Cultural Partnerships: Navigating the Complexities of Money and Mission*

PREFACE

As the subtitle of this book indicates, this is a "practical" guide. The themes assume certain unspoken theories and are influenced by my own natural biases, of course. There is also history, personal hindsight, and some optimistic idealism. It certainly draws on research, but mostly from personal experience. Therefore, the title of this book could be *Confessions of a Funding Recipient,* but it is about more than that. I'll explain. I served for nearly twenty years on a foreign mission field. Donor giving sustained my work. Then a job change caused me to spend time reflecting on mission workers' attitudes toward funding and the donors who give it.

Over the last several decades most parachurch mission workers did not receive a salary from the agency they served. Instead, they developed a personal donor base to cover their monthly living and work expenses. In addition, mission sending agencies helped their workers raise larger sums of money for special projects. The providers of those special funds, the postwar and Baby Boomer donors, were silent givers. They trusted the missionaries and their agencies to make good use of their donations because, after all, they were the experts.

I have always been conscientious about my own donor base. I depended on their giving to sustain my own missions work. Quarterly progress reports kept them informed, and good results kept them financially engaged. But there was another area that my colleagues on the field and I were not so good at: spending large sums of donor money we had raised for special projects.

I was pretty good at writing funding proposals. With the help of other team leaders, we were able to raise significant amounts of money for water projects, language surveys, equipment, training centers, and boat and auto purchases. We even helped provide the rationale for airplane purchases. The money was raised with few questions asked by the people reviewing our funding proposals.

Sometimes the money would arrive on the field only to remain in holding accounts for years with no expenditures. The idea behind certain projects seemed good at the time they were proposed, but steps toward implementing those ideas were never worked out. The people who would utilize the funds never arrived, or the reasons for the funding appeal were based on wrong assumptions. Donor-funded buildings were underutilized. Water projects failed soon after completion.

Because we were not personally connected with these sorts of donors, we assumed they would be okay with the mistakes, the wrong assumptions, and the poor planning.

When I started working with a funding organization as a funding proposal reviewer, I began to interact more directly with the donors. It turns out they were not so careless about the ineffective, if not wasteful, use of funds given to mission agencies. In fact, they took their ministerial role as donors quite seriously. They wanted to know how projects were progressing and about the problems the recipients faced. They were okay with mistakes—problems arise—but what were people doing to improve these situations? The donors usually didn't know because they were generally cut off from the discussions taking place on the field— discussions involving the use of their donor funds.

Getting to know the donors resulted in personal reflection over my attitude about them, their money, and their role in mission work. My hope is that this book will help funding proposal writers, people who make direct appeals for money, including church and ministry leaders, and those who spend that money consider the spiritual and ethical responsibility they bear before God and others in doing so.

I also hope that those who give the money will understand the complexities of ministry work under difficult circumstances and appreciate the unstable environments where the field workers live and serve, because even the best planning will need to deal with big challenges, seemingly on a regular basis.

Having covered confessions, let's move on to the goal of this book. It is meant as a guide to building effective partnerships between donors and funding recipients in mission and ministry. The donor may be a philanthropist or an entrepreneur. Or, the donor could be a church, a foundation, or an intermediary organization. The recipient may be a church, a private individual, or an organization working in the social or faith sector. Building a good working relationship between donor and recipient requires a refreshed understanding of each other's role. This kind of understanding is essential to a satisfying and lasting partnership.

Building an effective relationship is vital and perhaps even urgent. We live in a time of unprecedented opportunities for collaboration between donors and ministry workers. What makes our current context unique? The globalization of mission and ministry work in the twenty-first century has created a whole new set of dynamics. The center of Christianity has shifted to global southern regions. With this shift comes the mature and capable leadership of majority world leaders. These leaders are launching new ministry efforts in more places on an increasing scale and at an accelerating pace. Add to this the Western phenomenon of ten to forty trillion dollars currently changing hands from the Depression era generation to the Baby Boomer generation and their adult children, the Gen Xers. These Gen Xers are now giving an estimated 28.6 billion dollars annually in the USA (Bhagat, Loeb, and Rovner 2010). Even so, much more additional philanthropic wealth is still waiting in the wings.

Many of today's donors are reticent givers, and it is not because they lack generosity. This book addresses the factors contributing to their reticence. What can release their giving? The evidence indicates that donors will give to projects that have a clearly stated vision, are impact-oriented, have methods for monitoring and measuring progress, and build capacity among the people the ministry serves; all of this through partnership rather than independence.

Many funding recipients in the social and religious sector, however, have become accustomed to generous funding without thorough planning and accountability requirements. The increasingly sophisticated accountability donors are now requiring before giving is causing a significant degree of discomfort for many of the recipients. Frustration often grows among both parties. Recipients feel donors don't trust them, and donors feel recipients are not acting responsibly. Donors may also feel they don't have enough information to make wise decisions about their giving.

Time is running out for parachurch ministries and mission agencies, because donors are beginning to bypass their agencies. Now their funds are going directly to the church in Africa, Asia, Latin America, and the Pacific. Western agencies need to understand why this is happening. That requires reviewing historical patterns for why donors give to social projects and mission endeavors, and what happens to drive them and their money away.

What happened to the relationship between donors and the agencies they supported that resulted in so much tension and distrust between the two? How did the uncomplimentary term "donor-driven planning" come into use? And finally, why do many books urge donors to be more generous while so few challenge them to be effective givers? There are very few books or other resources that recognize the ministerial role of the donor and the biblical mandate for giving wisely and in a business-minded fashion. As one business person put it, the ministry they were giving to assumed "their role in God's mission was simply to pray, pay, and obey."

Much can also be said about the donors' need to understand how Christ's kingdom principles apply in the way they run their business and steward the extra funds that God has entrusted to them. I don't assume that business principles always align well with scriptural principles. However, there is already much written on that topic, therefore I defer to those authors who have covered that theme more effectively than I could in this volume.

The age of global giving is a time of reformation in mission and ministry funding. It appears that God is undoing the unbiblical division between the so-called laity and ministry, and he is also working through the new donors, among others, to improve the way workers carry out ministry and mission work.

This should not surprise us, given the rapid globalization of ministry, the decline of Western cross-cultural mission, and the realization that equal partnership is the only way that global mission can move forward. This latter notion was a major theme of the 2010 Third Lausanne Congress on World Evangelization in Cape Town. The gathering even produced a seven-page statement as an effort to improve the relationship between the donor and the funding recipient (The Lausanne Movement 2007).

The primary theme of this book focuses on emerging donor giving and behavior trends. Because it is trends analysis, most readers are able to mention current donor characteristics and behavior that contradict the trends described in this book. This is normal with a diachronic viewpoint. At the current rate of change, the emerging trends will become more of the norm sooner than perhaps people think.

This volume is only meant as an introduction to the topic of mission and ministry funding in the twenty-first century. Much more remains to be said on this topic. For now, my desire is for donors, social sector non-profits, mission agencies and local churches to gain a better understanding and appreciation of the role of the donor in mission and ministry these days. Additionally, may the donor see their role as ministerial rather than outside of mainstream ministry, as it has been perceived to be for so long. Hopefully, the information will generate more and better dialogue between both groups.

One thing is certain, as the innovation guru Seth Godin likes to say; the world does and is most certainly changing. These days, change is accelerating, so non-profit organizations that depend on donor funding will need to change more quickly. Because once again, money is moving to where it can have the greatest effect.

Acknowledgments

Any good outcomes from this volume belong to the donors, field workers, strategists, and implementers who taught me so much. In a big way, it also belongs to the people whom we are all trying to serve, because in the end, the degree to which their lives improve will judge how well we did in helping them.

A special thanks to the many people who kindly evaluated this manuscript, especially Susan Van Wynen, Johanna Fenton, Mary Lederleitner, Scott Anderson, Chuck DeVries, Samuel Chiang, Paul Edwards, Joe Class, Judy Sweeny, Micheal Occhipinti, and Andy Jones. Their comments, suggestions, and observations made it so much better. I take full responsibility for all of the content in this volume.

Over the course of writing, there were several people who, upon hearing about the topic, expressed how timely it is, and that is a strong form of encouragement.

Thank you to my wife, Gloria, who patiently endured many hours of me verbalizing my thoughts before writing.

Finally, I thank the individual donors and foundation leaders interviewed for this book. They are, as Dallas Willard said, practicing the true spirit of discipline, in relation to their wealth, their wisdom, and their experience.

I
THE ROLE OF THE DONOR:
A HISTORICAL VIEW

Jesus, Paul, and Money—A Modern Understanding
The financial donor's involvement in church planting ministry and missionary efforts had a simple beginning. Around the year AD 53, the Apostle Paul helped people in Corinth, Greece, set up their missions giving program. In a straightforward manner he instructed the individual church members to save a portion of money from their weekly wages. Then at the end of the month, they could all combine their donations into one large gift for missions.

This collection was not a mandatory Old Testament tithe, when giving a tenth of one's assets was strictly enforced by religious leaders. Paul stressed that each person was free to determine how much they could give based on their income level and probably other giving commitments too. Paul knew that the Corinthian church was a mosaic of social classes. Some of the church members were slaves, and some of them were quite well-to-do. There was also a middle class majority. The reason for the collection was simple. There were believers in Jerusalem who needed financial assistance and the Corinthian Christians were capable of helping, hence the first donor-recipient connection for the young church gathering.

Paul didn't explain in his written instructions to the Corinthian church how their donation would be used. It is clear that the money was for God's people in Jerusalem. House churches were springing up there, especially among the poor, so perhaps the Corinthians' giving would help strengthen that movement. This might also be the first time donors were asked to give money to the ministry on the assumption that the ministry workers would use it wisely and effectively. The amount was large enough to require a small group of people from the Corinthian church to deliver the generous load of coinage personally. Maybe the people bringing the donations planned on providing the due diligence for the Corinthian givers on how the Jerusalem believers planned to use that money. Therefore, the idea is made clear in those Bible passages that believers should use a portion of their funds for the greater good of the church. One could say that the Corinthian believers were the first missions project donors.[1]

Judging by their inclusion in a list of who's who in ministry, Paul revealed to the Roman church believers that people who give from their wealth were direct participants in mainstream church ministry (Rom 12:8). There was no clear indication that the list was given in order of importance, although beginning with prophet may hint of that. The role of providing financial help is fifth among seven important ministries described. Moreover, because this service was critical to the day-to-day life of the church, Paul urged the givers to carry out this ministry with serious intentions. Including the role of "giver" among other important ministry roles indicated that giving was not believed to be a separate department of the young church nor was it an adjunct to the more "spiritual" roles. Instead, the givers were co-ministers of the church. Not everyone had a surplus of money, therefore to have extra money seems to be meant as a spiritual gift from God for the functioning of the church.

Those passages in 1 Corinthians and Romans seem to indicate that God sovereignly creates wealth in certain individuals for his purposes. Are we reading too much into this? As we will see a little later, some wealthy people in history did indeed believe this was why they were blessed with the ability to make money, and lots of it. The important point to remember here is that giving away money was a ministry equal to other church ministries. Clearly, there was no division between the laity and the ministry at this point in time with respect to those who were gifted as generous givers.

---

1   Paul mentions in 1 Corinthians 16:1 that he instructed the Galatian believers to do the same, so they could be the first to function as ministry donors, rather than the Corinthians. Also, a few years before this, some of the Christians in Philippi and Macedonia assisted Paul financially with his missionary journeys. The Corinthian example seems to be the first organized effort of believers pooling their funds for the work of the church in other places.

The Apostle Paul was not the first person to talk about money in terms of spiritual matters. About twenty three years before that, Jesus had a lot to say about money, for example its joyful use, wise use, selfish use, sharing it, hoarding it, serving it, worshipping it, over-depending on it, and being deceived by it. This frequent topic should not be surprising, because much of his teaching was meant to help people attain peace, joy, and fulfillment in this life, and money then, as now, was a complicating factor in achieving that.

On more than one occasion, Jesus warned people about the shortsightedness of accumulating wealth without using it for the benefit of others. Jesus once told a story to point out that the accumulation of wealth was not the correct measure of a person's success in life. Instead, a person's true success was measured by the degree of beneficial impact their wealth had on other people. As the story goes, there was a rich person whose business was producing an enormous financial windfall. The man was gifted at making money, so much so that it was necessary for him to find creative ways to preserve it all. Then he could enjoy an early, secure, and comfortable retirement. What he didn't plan on was an early death, but that's what happened. He left all of his wealth stashed in various accounts with little to show for it. Sadly, that is how he would be remembered, even two thousand years later; a negative example of hoarding instead of helping.[2]

Whenever Jesus talked about money, he never condemned the making of money. Indeed, he never condemned people for having a lot of money, either. He mostly advised people with extra money to be generous towards people who had a demonstrable need for money. Perhaps his best known business and money analogy (according to my modern North American interpretation) is given in a story about an investor and a team of three fund managers. The investor gave a sum of money to each of the managers to invest. The amount of money each manager received was based on their level of investing skills. Sometime later, the investor was ready to sell off his holdings and take his profits, so he contacted the fund managers to ask them about his rate of return on each investment. The first fund manager was happy to report that his work yielded his client a 100 percent return on

---

2   Luke 12:18–21.

investment. The client was highly impressed, so he gave that fund manager twice the original amount to reinvest. Obviously, the manager was making a nice living off of the client, too.

The next fund manager was still somewhat new at investing, so the client had given him less money to work with. Even so, this manager reported that he also doubled the client's money. Seeing how the manager had demonstrated his ability as a shrewd and faithful investor, the client entrusted him with twice the amount he had given to him before. That came with a big raise in pay.

Finally, the last manager sent in his investment report. In the report, the manager informed his client that he was aware of his reputation as a serious investor. He knew that he didn't tolerate loses in the stock market nor did he tolerate fools. Because of this reputation, the manager was afraid to make a bad investment that could have resulted in a net loss for his client. Therefore, he simply put the money in a non-interest bearing bank account. He was happy to report that all of the client's money was still there, safe and sound.

The client was not stupid. He knew that inflation alone had already eaten away some of the value of his money. Instead of receiving the expected praise, the manager was severely scolded by the client for his bad performance. He sternly reminded the manager that he could have at least put the money in an interest-bearing account and made even a little bit of profit. Therefore, he fired the manager and transferred the investment funds to the first manager who had doubled his money. He also made sure that the bad manager could never work in the investment industry again or enjoy the benefits of that work.

There are a few important takeaways from this modern rephrasing of the parable of the talents,[3] but one point is particularly clear. Essentially, Jesus gave his audience a stern warning. He told them that no matter what God has entrusted to people, whether it is a little or a lot, insignificant or important, he fully expects them to be wise in how they use what they have been given. Resources are given so that more good can come from them.

---

3   A talent was a unit of measure of probably gold or silver.

And those who keep the resources for themselves risk losing it all, even if it is just a small thing. The good news is that people who are wise and faithful managers of what they have been given will be honored with more, but only to be reinvested for the even greater good.[4]

Pastors and theologians have applied this money metaphor to all sorts of situations in life and ministry, and admittedly, my business culture interpretation may not be shared by others. Even so, a salient point of Jesus' teaching seems to be that God sovereignly gives things for his purposes, and he has the sovereign right to take things away—and he does! Applying a financial stewardship interpretation, apparently being a generous giver is only half of the responsibility of having extra money. It appears that the wise and shrewd management of that money is the other half. How have the givers and the church in general done with this principle over the ages?

Ministry and Money—The Donor on the Outside

In the earliest days of the church, believers who associated with various church gatherings were called on to use some of their funds for the benefit of the church. The first recorded funding appeal in the New Testament was meant to assist newly planted churches in other places. This pattern went on for another 1,700 years and so the church grew and spread throughout Africa, Asia, and Europe.

By the eighteenth century, Europe had become largely a Christian land, but efforts to spread the gospel to the rest of the world were still rather limited. Protestant denominations were beginning to form, and most of them formed for good reasons. They were attempting to address a doctrinal imbalance or rectify areas of neglect in ministry or society. Even so, a negative side effect of these adjustments was schisms. Rather than developing cooperative ways of working together, the denominations often created divisions and barriers to cooperation.

It was also during this time that the Old Testament concept of "tithing"— giving one tenth of one's income to the church—had become common practice. The practice seems to have neglected the Apostle Paul's teachings

---

4   Matthew 25:14–28.

on giving as described in his first letter to the church in Corinth. Now giving was based on a simple, mathematically defined Old Testament formula. Furthermore, in many churches, the church hierarchy or administration decided how to spend the money. Some of the funds were for starting more churches, but only churches that preserved and promoted the doctrinal particularities of the denomination. As one church historian commented, it seems that at this point in time the church shifted from being outwardly focused to self-regarding (Walls 2005, 16). More and more of the givers' money was used internally to maintain a growing church infrastructure and budget, and less was applied directly outside of the church budget for expanding the gospel and alleviating pressing social problems.

These Protestant denominations were not always the most concerned with spreading the gospel to the uttermost parts of the earth.[5] William Carey, the purported father of modern Protestant mission, was part of the young Baptist Church movement in England. He felt a strong calling to bring the gospel to India. However, his denomination was not interested in sending him there or anywhere else, so he ingeniously invented an organization that would. He formed a missionary society. The society's members were volunteers and its economic engine was made up of lower, middle, and upper class donors. The society resembled the Corinthian church mentioned earlier in that everyone was contributing in various ways according to their ability. One could say the missionary society movement birthed what later became known as the "parachurch movement."

The term "parachurch" describes how the mainline church viewed the missionary society's work. The prefix "para" can be translated as "on the fringe" or "alongside of," and fringe in this usage means "less than." For example, a paralegal is not a full-fledged lawyer and a paramedic is not a full-fledged doctor, and that seems appropriate. With the established church, however, the prefix carried a "you're not fully a part of mainstream church ministry" stigma. In other words, the beginning of the modern

---

5   Neill commented that one thing the denominations did agree on was that they, the Anglicans, Methodists, and Baptists, comprised the worldwide Christian fellowship, instead of seeing themselves as they actually were, an imperfect and fragmented incorporation in the body of Christ (Neill 1964, 514).

Protestant mission movement was considered to be a side show of the church carried out by volunteers, not ministers. The missionary society concept worked for Carey because he became their first missionary.

People are so accustomed to the existence of parachurch organizations that they don't realize how radically disruptive the movement was to the mainstream church in its earliest days.[6] Soon other innovative thinkers operating on the fringe of mainstream church ministry began to launch other missionary societies, and these societies were the primary channel for sending missionaries to far flung places. Now people from different denominations could more easily work together. It was truly a grassroots movement. They could innovate, develop programs, and raise funds specifically for launching foreign missionary endeavors, even though ministerial Christianity had not given them "permission" to do so.[7] This is when the donor-recipient model in missions began to flourish. The donors were individuals raising money or giving from their own income, and the recipients were the societies or the missionaries they sent out. This direct involvement in missions by the donor was a source of meaning and satisfaction in their lives. At this time, the donors were still "insiders," so they knew how the society would apply those funds.

The Division Widens

By the eighteenth century, religious training was usually obtained through seminaries that were typically part of a university. Schools like Oxford in England and Yale and Harvard in the United States were significantly equipping people for full time ministry, and church denominations were forming their own seminaries as well, so now ministers of the gospel could be ordained through this sort of education. People who served the church but who were not ordained were called the laity, meaning "the people at large." As a result of this shift, the various ministry roles the Apostle Paul outlined in his letter to the Roman and Corinthian churches were now

---

6 Walls provides a vivid description of this time in history revealing how truly radical these grassroots movers and shakers for missions were (1988).

7 By the twentieth century, most missionaries had some sort of official link with a church, but in earlier times a missionary's only means of support was a missionary society. Granted, some were separatist for doctrinal reasons too.

divided along two lines. The role of apostle and pastor were "professional" ministries of sorts and the other roles were typically carried out by the laity. Therefore, the other ministry roles described by Paul were now considered to be on the margin of these other ministry roles, which came to be viewed as "core" ministry. Eventually, the giver would miss the cut altogether and become simply the donor—a source of funds for the ministry, the laity, and the missionary society.

Soon after Carey launched his parachurch organization, the mainline church denominations were beginning to increase overseas. Many followed on the heels of their government's colonialist expansion, and their mission was to establish a denominational presence in those countries. No doubt many of their ministers sincerely cared about reaching the local people with the gospel through their church presence. Their economic engine was the home church and the tithes collected from its members.

It sounds a little cynical to think that the home church office was only interested in controlling their denominational churches in those places. Still, as missiologist and mission historian Samuel Escobar put it, the expansion of mainline churches overseas was much like a modern business franchise, and a franchise brand had to be guarded lest the whole denomination be tainted by one problematic church. Therefore funding from the home office was one way to control the denomination's brand through the use of funding, or the lack thereof (Escobar 2003, 134–35). And as the home church went, so went its overseas churches. The eventual decline in mainline church missions funding was in no small way a result of the tithers beginning to act like shrewd givers by investing their money in other places, such as parachurch ministries.

Another mark of the early parachurch or missionary society movement was the development of entrepreneurial enterprises to fund the mission. Religious entrepreneurship was not just for the wealthy. Supporters of the missionary societies were committed to entrepreneurship as their economic engine for launching and sustaining the overseas work. That meant, among other things, enrolling volunteers to produce simple goods, such as pot holders and quilts that could be sold for cash. It also meant starting small businesses that produced enough financial profit to augment the cash needs of the societies. Once again, these entrepreneurs were not an official part of ministry, but they were still fully participating in church ministry, even if it was believed to be on the fringe of mainline ministry at the time.

In Germany, the Moravians became well known for their grassroots entrepreneurship purely for the sake of sending as many missionaries as they could to some of the most remote places on earth at the time. Not all overseas missionary society efforts were successful, though. Some of them failed miserably. Still, by the mid-nineteenth century the missionary societies, fueled by their entrepreneurial activities and aided by philanthropists, could be credited with sending thousands of missionaries overseas. By 1915 one North American society called the Student Volunteer Movement for Foreign Missions had sent four thousand volunteer missionaries to various countries (Escobar 2003, 50). The missionary society movement was, by and large, the work of the laity, the people who, without any official standing in the church, took it upon themselves to do what they believed the mission of the church to be: spreading the gospel to ever more places, away from the heartland and into the hinterlands. And the entrepreneurial-minded donors (the givers) provided the economic strength that allowed this movement to flourish.

The Emergence of "Donor-driven" Mission Planning

It is no surprise that missionary society volunteers displayed such entrepreneurial behavior for the sake of missionary society support. After all, the late 1700s through the late 1800s was a golden age for philanthropy. In Europe and America, wealthy business people were pouring their own money into solving some of the most pressing social needs of the time. They often applied the same creative and innovative thinking that produced much of their wealth in the first place (Bishop and Green 2008, 13–29). They wanted to alleviate suffering and create programs that could help lift people out of poverty, and they brought common sense business thinking to their social and religious programs to accomplish that. Many of them were not interested in simply handing their money over to a charity or a poorly defined social cause, especially one that lacked sound planning. As business people they valued programs that produced sustainable growth.

They abhorred waste and desired to see greater effects. They treated their investments in producing social capital the same as they did in a business venture. That is, to have the greatest return possible. And that return on investment could then be reinvested to create even more social good. Were these people aware of Jesus' teaching about the three fund managers, our modern version of the parable of the talents?

One such entrepreneur was Arthur Guinness. He was the founder of the Guinness beer brewing empire of Dublin, Ireland. Arthur was a devout Christian. In the late 1700s, he was attending one of the first Evangelical churches in Ireland where personal Bible reading and study were encouraged. Could it have been during one of those Bible readings when Arthur first understood his role as Paul's Romans 12:8 "givers" or the shrewd money manager that Jesus described? He believed God had gifted him with the making of money precisely for the purpose of serving God and society with that money. This gifting would eventually produce enormous good for the masses of impoverished people living in what was then referred to as Ireland's Calcutta (Mansfield 2009). The money would also be used to help establish orphanages and plant churches all over the world. Moreover, Arthur believed it was important to expand his beer brewing business precisely so that he could increase his philanthropic work.

By the late 1800s, philanthropists were increasingly viewed with suspicion by the mainstream church and especially the mission implementers because they were not officially part of church ministry. To make matters worse, their "ministry" language was that of Enlightenment period philanthropy and business rather than that of biblical theology, so their philanthropic activities seemed even less church-like than ever. Yet, this didn't prevent some philanthropists from asserting leadership in matters of the church, particularly in its overseas mission work. No doubt, some of them exercised poor judgment in giving to causes which resulted in waste. People tend to remember failure more keenly than success, and that didn't help philanthropists' role in ministry then, nor does it now. Even so, there were some wealthy contributors who stood out as innovative thinkers in the realm of money and mission.

Robert Arthington (1823–1864) was called "a rich friend of missions" by one church historian because he eventually gave 90 percent of his wealth to missionary endeavors (Walls 1990, 13). The label "friend" infers that he was not a missionary, nor did he hold any ministerial position in the church. He was part of the laity; in this case a financial donor. Even so, he had strong opinions on where the British Missionary Society should launch their first African mission effort and how they should use the funds he provided for that mission work. He persuaded them to work in Zaire first, even though they were thinking of starting work in another place. He also placed a large sum of money in a trust fund to be used after he died. However, the funds could only be used to start new work, even if the missionaries were running a deficit with their current work.

His giving conditions forced them to be more fiscally minded, probably through better planning. The mission implementers were glad to receive Arthington's money, but they were not happy about his influence on their society's work. Yet, he was well read, knew a lot about Africa, and cared much about the spiritual needs of the people. He was well informed and thus more capable of applying due diligence in his giving (Stanley 1998). He wanted to make sure his giving would enable mission expansion, even to the shores of Lake Tanganyika, for the greatest possible impact.

No doubt, not all wealthy givers to mission endeavors have been so well-informed. Some of them probably drove mission agendas in ways that resulted in wasting money and time. But mission history seems to have lumped the wise givers with the not-so-wise givers and usually warns of the latter while not acknowledging the value of the former.

Profile of a Twenty-first-century Giver

John is a gifted thinker and problem solver. His creativity has enabled him to generate significant wealth, and the majority of it is to benefit mission and ministry work. Along with success, he has also learned some hard lessons from his own business ventures that resulted in wasted money. After donating and visiting mission agency headquarters and studying what they were doing, "It was like viewing government spending. I cannot believe they would spend money like this."

He didn't want to change their mission organization. He just wanted to help them with business management and fund raising. He wanted the denominational ministries and parachurch organizations to figure out how to make more disciples through improved business and accountability models. Therefore, he sought opportunities to discuss his ideas with their leaders. Even though he understood their mission model, his layman role had resulted in them being more interested in his substantial giving than his well-formed ideas.

By the end of the nineteenth century, John D. Rockefeller would echo the same sentiments as Arthur Guinness and Robert Arthington. He believed God had gifted him to make money and that large amounts of that money could be used for the good of others. By the age of sixteen, Rockefeller was already contributing carefully and thoughtfully to a number of charities and causes (Brooks 2002, 38). He also had some concerns over churches' and charities' apparent inability to produce greater sustainable outcomes. The philanthropic behavior of Carnegie and Rockefeller would influence other highly capable givers, including current philanthropists like Bill Gates and Warren Buffett. With Gates, generosity for social good is a principle he learned from his parents (Bishop and Green 2008, 31). Apparently, neither Gates nor Buffett want to store all of their wealth in banks where it is lost through lack of good use, as Jesus' teaching reminds us.

Although the philanthropists of earlier times did not hold missionary or ministerial positions in the mainline church or parachurch ministry—indeed some of them were not even professing believers—clearly they were using their wealth to benefit the poor in ways in which Jesus said personal wealth should be used. That is, they invested it in order to bring about a greater return. In this case, it was a greater return on building social capital for the common good of society, especially society's poor.

Because these philanthropists were viewed as outside of main stream ministry, some ministers ascribed impure motives for their involvement in the social and religious sectors. One recent author even suggested that nineteenth-century American philanthropists, such as Dale Carnegie and John D. Rockefeller, were only motivated by capitalism. That is to say, their investments in the social sector were only out of a desire to create more consumers who could generate more wealth for their own industries. It is as if they were only investing in their own future consumer markets to produce more profits for themselves.

To suggest their motives for giving generously were purely self-serving is hubris.[8] It is true that throughout history some involved in philanthropic efforts have done it by generating wealth in ways that were not just or fair to their workers. Capitalism without a social conscience has produced more harm than good, even when these sorts of philanthropists give away large sums of money. However, many others have generated profound quantities of wealth in ways that created opportunities and just work environments for employees.

Even if the philanthropists were unaware of Jesus' teaching, many of them were motivated by the same principles he taught in the parable of the talents, which is making the best use of money for the greatest returns. In the business sector, this mentality certainly had some harmful effects on common people at times, but in the social sector it brought much improved planning, management, and evaluation for greater results, and society benefited.

The behavior of people like Arthington and Rockefeller is an early example of a growing lack of trust between the donor and the denominational mission agency. The agency believed they knew best how to spend the donor's money, but the donors were beginning to doubt the ability of the agency to make sound plans and produce good results with those funds. Indeed, by

---

8   Willmer's assessment of Carnegie's giving motives seems judgmental and predisposed because of Carnegie's views and sociology language at the time (Willmer 2008, 28–29). Arthur Brooks, the author of *Who Really Cares* (2002, 26), also questions such dismissive judgments over the giving motives of this era's philanthropist. Ideological differences may exist, but the principles of benefiting society with extra wealth, rather than hoarding it, is the central point and relates to Jesus' teaching on this topic.

this time the division between the ministry and the laity mentioned earlier became even sharper in regard to the donor's role in missions and ministry. There was little recognition that both the donor and the mission agency had knowledge and experience gaps that the other could fill as co-workers of the gospel. In Arthington's case, he was the generous giver who also happened to be a shrewd investor in the business sector. He believed God had entrusted him to make shrewd investments with his wealth for greater returns in the spiritual realm. The other laborers were the missionaries. They had the tenacity and sense of calling to bring the gospel to such dangerous unreached places as the Congo river basin. In a sense, they were also investors, but of their time, skills, and wisdom for the greatest good.

As a result of the growing tension between donor and doer, the agencies began to view the kind of control that Arthington, and others after him, brought to mission work as "donor-driven mission." It is not seen as a positive term. It often implies that the donor is meddling in things they presumably know nothing about. Even so, the agency needed donor funds to carry out their work, but more donors wanted to have a say in the mission plan, so over time funding increasingly came with requirements. Moreover, the growing influence of Marxism and Socialism by the mid-1900s began to paint capitalism and business practices in a bad light, selectively focusing on cases of clear abuse rather than those of true benevolence. As a result, the mainline church and mission agencies gained a greater distaste for any kind of business influence on what they perceived to be purely spiritual work. At least, who was tasked to do the spiritual work of the church became more narrowly defined.

By the mid-twentieth century, parachurch missionary work continued to grow and funding for those efforts increased as well. At the same time, member giving to mainline churches was declining.[9] As mentioned earlier, mainline church foreign mission work was affected by the financial health of the home church. Now donors were beginning to vote with their money,

---

9   See Vallet and Zech 1995. For the United States, they list the United Church of Christ, Episcopal Church, Presbyterian Church, American Baptist Church, Christian Church (Church of Christ), Evangelical Lutheran Church (USA), Reformed Church, and United Methodist Church as mainline.

and the mainline church seemed to be on the losing end, with both the home church and their missionaries feeling the effects. Cutbacks became necessary. Previously, church member giving did not affect income, because the givers simply trusted church leadership with the use of those funds. But now the distrust that wealthy philanthropists had of the mainline churches' use of their financial gifts even began to spread to the average middle-class giver.

During earlier times, mainline church members gave to a general benevolence fund. That fund was used for ministry work outside of the church, and the foreign mission work received their income from this source. Typically, most of the people giving to the benevolence fund had no idea how the funds were used. But by the late twentieth century, the people who gave money for church and mission work were becoming dissatisfied with the results of their giving. They saw a growing internal church infrastructure that required more money to maintain, so funds for foreign missions and other external ministry work remained static, if not reduced.

The emergence of the Baby Boomer generation had no small impact on the shift of giving to the parachurch. A mark of that generation was a general distrust of institutions, especially large ones with low accountability. As young, thinking adults, they developed a growing concern over their churches' use of mission giving and the paternalistic or even neo-colonialistic behavior they believed was attached to those funds. Previously, church member contributions were given out of a sense of duty or obligation; however, these younger donors did not share that sense of obligation. They were unwilling to give blindly to a church as a whole, much less a department of a church. Instead, they wanted to participate in achieving a preferably clear cause, such as planting *x* number of churches in India or completing Bible translation projects in Africa. The benevolence giving model was no longer satisfying them. Actually, they viewed it with suspicion.

As a result of this growing distrust and disengagement, there was a marked shift to donor-designated giving. This way the donors knew where their money was going and how it would be generally used. But their knowledge of the projects they gave to was still somewhat superficial. They were not asking many questions about measurable outcomes and impacts.

Indeed, regular quality reporting to the donors on the mission's endeavors wasn't even standard in the financial relationship. Even so, the donors were increasingly aware of how their giving was theoretically affecting positive change, so donor-designated giving became more satisfying to them than previous giving methods. This shift is not unique to the Western mainline church. The Korean Presbyterian church has also seen a similar trend (Lee 2011, 222–39).

Giving structures of the mainline church probably unintentionally contributed to the growth in donor-designated giving to parachurch ministries. This is because there was no system in place to allow the mainline church givers to indicate their wishes for how their financial gifts could be used. With some church denominations it was an affront to the ministry for the person giving the money to suggest how the ministry should use those funds. The donor's questions or suggestions were viewed as naïve at best or meddling at worst. Because they were "just" lay people, they presumably didn't know how to apply the money in appropriate ways. Even if their suggestions were expressed in naïve terms, the hierarchical structure didn't typically allow for open dialogue in the use of ministry money.

As a result of this shift, by the late twentieth century the donors were beginning to join forces with grassroots missions and ministries. This was similar to what had happened in the earliest days of the Protestant Church mission movement. Now more donors were becoming convinced they could do a better job in determining good use of church mission and ministry funds than church bureaucracy could. Their designated giving was at least providing them with a feeling of greater involvement in the mission projects. This kind of involvement also provided ease of conscience before God over how they were using his money.

Profile of a Twenty-first-century Giver

Clint is a very capable financial giver. Using his creative and innovative giftings, he built a nationally acclaimed human resource consulting company. He wants to give more of his financial resources to his local church, but he has concerns over the elders' lack of clarity in how they will impact the community with those funds. He is reticent to ask for more details because earlier attempts to do so did not go well with the elders. They believe he should just give generously in accordance with his ability and let them determine the use of the money. They also feel they should not show preference to one person just because of the large amount of his giving. Clint wants to help, but as a wise businessman he is concerned that his giving will not have far-reaching effects. If not preferential, could ministry leaders be deferential to major givers like Clint as co-ministers by inviting their comments on ministry planning or at least seeking their input on the elders' ideas, considering the level of their financial giving and their business experience?

2
DISSECTING THE STATUS QUO

A Renewal of Giving as Mainstream Ministry
Could the shift to donor-designated giving have anything to do with theological reflection by the more idealistic Baby Boomer generation? By the 1970s, the donors were beginning to act more like wise stewards rather than "leave-it-to-the-experts" givers. Now "stewardship," rather than "benevolence," was becoming the operating word within the parachurch. Pastor and author Dallas Willard wrote, "Stewardship—which requires possessions and includes giving—is the true spirit of discipline in relation to wealth." He goes on to remind the reader that feeling guilty over having possessions has no place in scriptural faith, and guilt for having wealth may actually be a hindrance to its right use. Instead, he asserts that "material wealth is a spiritual service of the highest order" (Willard 1988, 194).

Much has been written, usually by fundraising professionals, on why wealthy donors should be generous in their giving. They spend much time spelling out the theological basis for it. They sometimes explain that giving generously is for the donor's own spiritual transformation, and that is certainly true. But it seems that little is ever said about how the donor should operate as a wise giver. This follows a long-term pattern of fundraising professionals assuming donors would not be informed enough to serve as a sounding board on their organization's plans and strategies before making a funding appeal. At best, it is simply because of traditional mindsets. At worst, it is because of the recipients' fear over the negative effects such openness could have on a donor's giving decision.

The separation of the laity from the ministry, discussed in chapter 1, also resulted in fundraisers only seeking after a donor's money rather than his knowledge, insights, wisdom, and expertise, which could contribute to the work of the ministry. These are the things that made the donors successful enough to give generously in the first place. Stewardship is more than just being a generous source of money for church, missions, and ministries. Spiritual transformation of the donor also means learning how to be wise and shrewd in their giving in order to influence ministries in beneficial ways. A donor, however, acting wisely or shrewdly in their giving has often been interpreted by the recipient as meddling.

As mentioned in the previous section, when donors do attempt to act wisely or shrewdly with their giving, they usually do that through questions. They might make suggestions from a business person's point of view using business terminology. Commonly, the ministry workers refer to this as donor-driven planning. Some of them may even react to the donor's non-theological language. Today, as in the past, because of ministry personnel's reluctance to partner well, some donors are uninformed over the realities of ministry, especially as it pertains to work on the mission field, so their questions may indeed sound naïve. Even so, it is often the pastors' and missionaries' wrong view of the role of the donor in ministry that has resulted in this historic tension, stemming from the donor's money and their questions that occasionally come with it.[10]

The Donor-Recipient Division Dissected

A significant reason for the breakdown in the donor-recipient relationship is that mainstream ministry has not typically viewed the donors as co-ministers of the gospel. Yet, that is precisely who the Apostle Paul and some modern theologians, such as Dallas Willard, consider them to be. Even the donors do not generally view themselves in that way, because they are used to being on the outside. Yet, ironically it was the entrepreneurial givers who had a core role in sending out missionaries and funding social causes, much more so than the mainstream church did.

---

10 During my current ten-year long tenure working on the ministry funding side of things, I have become accustomed to hearing ministry workers voice their disdain over donors asking questions and making suggestions to project funding recipients.

About two hundred years after the modern missions movement began (and nearly two thousand years after Paul described the giver's role in ministry), the role of the giver—the modern day financial donor—seems to be coming on strong in this era, the early part of the twenty-first century. Could God be re-establishing the role of giving generously as a core role in ministry? Is the church waking up to how God intended it to operate from the beginning? Perhaps a brief review of how the givers gave as well as their reasons for giving over the last few hundred years will help donor and funding recipients to understand the times they now live in. A simplified way of seeing these changes is by retracing the vocabulary of giving, as we have already begun to do in this section.

The Language of Giving through the Ages

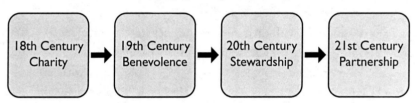

| 18th Century Charity | 19th Century Benevolence | 20th Century Stewardship | 21st Century Partnership |

CHARITY

The term "charity" was in common use during the eighteenth century. It is from the Latin word *caritas,* "Christian love." The greatest gift, as the Apostle Paul wrote in Greek to the Corinthian church, was *agape,* "love." Giving to needy causes was one way for Christians to show love. Many charities existed in Europe and North America, and broad appeals were made to help fund these charities. Typically, individuals gave directly to the charities. The average donor's knowledge of needs in the world at this time was still rather limited to the information communicated by the charities.

BENEVOLENCE

Charitable giving became more institutionalized in the nineteenth century in the mainline church. That is, mission and ministry became departments of the church. Church members were directed to give to the church benevolence fund for these programs. The definition of "benevolence" describes giving as an act of good will or kindness. By this time, however, some givers began to view this term more of a euphemism for funding the churches' programs (Vallet and Zech 1995, chapters 1–2). This removed the donors from having direct contact or involvement with the recipients. Yet, by this time the donors had a greater understanding of the need for evangelism and establishing churches, and they made use of the benevolence offering to address those needs.

STEWARDSHIP

By the mid-twentieth century, there was more common knowledge of people, places, and difficult situations in the world. This was due to increased literacy, rapid communications, ocean and air transportation, and in no small way, because of two world wars.

With increased knowledge comes increased accountability, so donors began to wonder about the effects their church was having on these local and global situations with their giving. They began to speak of being better stewards of the money God had given to them. The term "steward" means to watch over or manage something, and this is how they saw themselves. They began taking more personal spiritual responsibility in managing the money that God had entrusted to them for the benefit of others. The shift in terminology at this time signaled a return to Jesus' core teaching on shrewdly stewarding the things that God had given to them. As a result, donor giving to parachurch ministries and mission agencies began to increase. Stewardship also brought performance benchmarks and other accountability practices attached to grants, often to the annoyance of the ministry workers.

The Methods of Giving over the Centuries

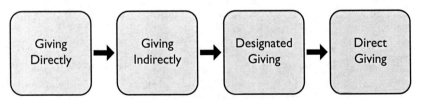

Now signs indicate a return to the direct giving patterns of earlier times, but now globally rather than just locally. In fact, according to recent research, direct donations now exceed all other ways of giving among all four generations—Gen Y, Gen X, Boomers, and Matures (Bhagat, Loeb, and Rovner 2010).

Websites that make it easy to give directly are flourishing. Kickstarter was one of the first online fundraising sites to provide a way for anyone to set up a fundraising campaign. The website is used by a variety of people for a variety of reasons. Not all of the giving opportunities on Kickstarter are for social sector or faith-based work. However, people from these sectors are using Kickstarter to generate direct giving to their causes. This direct fundraising and direct giving platform has sparked interest among others to do the same. Now organizations like GiveDirectly make it possible for donors to give cash directly to the people who need it most, bypassing corrupt government handlers and inefficient agencies.

However, direct giving is not necessarily effective giving if the donor doesn't know much about who they are giving to or how their giving is really helping people. Organizations like GiveWell exist to provide in-depth research for direct givers. Phone giving apps (donation software) for direct and immediate giving abound as well. The concept of software-driven direct giving is catching on. Consider sisterindia.org. Passionate about faith-based mission work in India, one donor launched his own direct giving website. He invited his friends to participate by giving to a project on the site or by starting their own giving campaign on the same site, as long as it benefited women's literacy training in India.

These are only a few examples of the hundreds of direct giving sites cropping up each year. On the surface, this trend is symptomatic. People are increasingly dissatisfied with the status quo of giving through an agency. Middleman agencies can provide a lot of help. They can ensure effective giving. They can help the donor to achieve greater success in their giving. But middleman agencies separate the donor from the recipient. Certainly, a website is a kind of middleman, connecting the giver with the recipient, but the service is much more in the background, almost unnoticeable. The faces you see on the website are the very people you help. It is not the face of an agency fundraiser or an organization's president. It feels more direct, even if it isn't any more direct than giving through an agency.

Direct giving through a website makes people feel like they have more control of their giving. It provides, for the giver at least, immediate impact. How well their funds are used by the recipient is something that few really think about. Ken Sterns, the author of *With Charity for All*, points out how this sort of giving is understandable because it meets a need in people to make a difference without investing a lot of time (Stern 2013). These sorts of donors don't think about how much difference they actually make. That would require more work. As easy as it is to raise funds that bring immediate donor satisfaction, Sterns admonishes fundraising agencies, which presumably includes direct giving websites, to help givers enjoy more long-term satisfaction by also coaching them on effective giving.

Direct giving Websites and software apps appear to be one way to fill the need to make a difference, and that more personally because of the direct connection. Chapter 6 discusses how to give directly and effectively. For now, it is important to understand that direct giving is not just a short-lived trend, but a framework change in how people give.

The trend is clear. Western donors (individuals and agencies) giving directly to foreign nationals working in their own country increased 183 percent from 1996 to 2005 (Moreau 2008, 4). However, this shift is causing a reduction in the number of Western workers sent to traditional missionary receiving countries. For example, a megachurch in Southern California reduced the number of missionaries they supported from sixty to just twelve. The funds they used to spend sending and maintaining missionaries overseas are now going directly to local church ministries run by Kenyans, Congolese, and Sri Lankan people in their countries.

Profile of a Twenty-first-century Giver

Peter and Gail don't see their ministry as one-dimensional, i.e., just about giving money. They have the gift of generosity, but they also have other gifts to offer, such as mercy, wisdom, and encouragement. God gives gifts to individuals that allow them to be successful in business and make money, but one shouldn't separate their spiritual gifts from their money. Giving is only a part of the equation.

One pattern emerging from this change is a possible correspondence between the donor's knowledge of the pressing spiritual and material needs in the world and their response to that knowledge. That is, they are acting on what they know. This increased focus on being both an active partner and a wise financial steward is creating a new force in twenty-first-century mission. The children of the Baby Boomer generation are now becoming the donors of ministry and missions in the early part of the third millennium. They are more impatient with waste, weak planning, and poor returns on giving than their parents were. They have generally achieved faster success through more creative methods in their own work. They may define success and good outcomes differently, as well, with less focus on numbers and more on relationships, holistic ministry, and impact.[11] How will the ministry view this new breed of donor? The characteristics of these donors and their role in ministry will be covered in chapter 5.

The Business of Mission

The church mission historian and missiologist Andrew Walls had some particularly sharp criticism of American methodology in mission that might surprise many of those missionaries. His critique was that "it stands for an uninhibited approach to money and a corresponding concern with size and scale . . . American missions are thus both products and purveyors of American culture" (Walls 1990, 3). Another missiologist, who apparently agrees with Walls, believes that such practice is often because of donor influence. His point is that the influence was "an attempt to turn Christian Mission into a managerial enterprise . . . Missionary action is translated into logical steps to be followed in a process of management by objectives" (Escobar 1991, 11). Is there any truth to their criticism?

Western donors, particularly Americans, tend to bring what Mark Knoll described as a methodological common sense approach to ministry (Noll 1985, 216–38). A major argument of this book is that being wise and shrewd with money, as any good business person should be, is indeed a theological imperative. This view of ministry is part of American evangelical

---

11 From the Greek word *holos* "all, entire," rather than from the English word "whole," hence the spelling choice here.

church culture. Yet, sometimes applying common sense business principles to ministry work can turn into a demanding and misdirected end in itself. This can force the ministry partners to focus on the wrong things. They may feel compelled to achieve faster or greater results, usually documented numerically. Also, donor expectations for greater outcomes than can be reasonably achieved within a stated time frame can cause mission planners to over-plan. This approach also has to do with changed numbers rather than changed lives. Even in mission work, a growth plan should be based on what is realistically possible at any given time.

It is not worldly to apply good planning in any ministry endeavor. Jesus said something about that with regard to discipleship, and the planning illustration he used seems apt for mission and ministry, too.[12] After all, shouldn't ministries strive for excellence in what they do so that God is glorified in plain view of the non-believing world? Even so, striking a balance between excellence and dominance has its challenges. When the balance tips to domineering, the mission business model becomes an end in itself rather than a way to develop people who can carry out and expand ministry efforts. By this point, things are indeed out of balance. An over-emphasis on business plans with unrealistic goals can cause one to lose sight of the ultimate goal. Sometimes donors are guilty of this overemphasis.

Money as an Input, Not an End

There is some truth to Walls' comment. In the past, some donors believed funding alone, and lots of it, could generate rapid and greater success in ministry outcomes. Hindsight reveals that abundant funding did not always achieve what it was meant to. In spite of it, ministry projects still took years to complete. Many never finished. Buildings were constructed but never used. New ministry efforts were launched, but they did not last long. A lot of money was wasted. Indeed, the weakest part of this strategy was leaving the affected people out of the planning process.

Doing things "for" people, using money as the primary instrument, is another balance concern. When you spend money on people rather than

---

12 Luke 14:28–29.

with them, they do not always receive the benefit of being trained and equipped to launch, nurture, and sustain their own ministry work. Instead, they view the project as belonging to either the donor or the ministry. The pressure to rapidly spend large sums of money tends to leave people out of the planning process because of the presumed inefficiency of including them. Sometimes, large cash infusions to address a need or accelerate a plan result in hurting more than helping. The donor's desire to give large sums of money as a methodology in itself is unwise.

Spending Money

Applying funding to something other than what the donor assumed or specified it would be used on has been a common source of tension between donor and ministry. A designated gift was expected to be used for one thing, and the ministry ended up using it for something else. Although this is illegal with American accounting practices, ministry recipients can be naïve about designated funds requirement. For some workers, as long as it is applied to the ministry work, shifting funds to another priority seems aboveboard. For example, a donor gave money to a mission agency for flying their ministry worker to various project locations. The donor believed flying was an efficient way to cover more projects in a short amount of time. He thought this was an efficient use of his financial gift because it could produce results sooner. Nevertheless, the ministry worker was operating from a different cultural context, one that has more time than money. Therefore, he chose to use overland transportation instead, because he felt it was wasteful to spend that much money on air travel, even if it meant taking longer to reach the project locations. As far as he understood, he was still applying it to travel. Both the donor and the ministry worker had equally valid concerns, but the donor's lack of clarity in understanding the project's cultural context resulted in strained relationships. Their failure to communicate their reasons for giving to a travel fund, and particularly for funding air travel, would have helped to avoid this misunderstanding, even if they assumed the recipient understood their desires and Western accounting practices.

More commonly, donors give to causes assuming that ministry workers will implement a well-thought-out plan. For example, a donor gave a substantial amount of money to a ministry that works with troubled young people. The ministry wanted to build a weekend camp and counseling center for them. Nearly six months passed and the donor had not received any reports on how the construction was going, so he decided to enquire about it. His contact responded that the higher level leaders in the organization had determined that the camp was not needed after all, so they spent the money on other ministry efforts. And because that money would still benefit the youths, they assumed that would be okay with the donor. The donor was disappointed with their response, mostly because they left him out of the information loop. Even so, instead of feeling offended and cutting off any future funding, he decided next time he would first be more diligent in investigating how well they had thought out their plans before providing a grant. Before making a funding appeal, this ministry had not done their own due diligence to determine if the project was actually needed. On the other hand, the donor's naïve trust exacerbated the problem.

The point of this story is that donors are busy people and sometimes they give too quickly. With the latter example, this led the donor to believe the ministry worker had not respected his reason for giving, even though it benefited another area of the ministry. Weak due diligence on the part of the donor often results in these sorts of situations. Donors are also accountable for their inaction in this area.

Controlling with Money

A neo-colonialist attitude in giving has not generally been a mark of the Boomer generation as perhaps it was with previous generations. Still, some funders in current times have applied their giving with this mentality. Simply defined, neo-colonialism means to control the situation in a foreign land through other means now that one no longer has colonial powers. This way of thinking also breeds paternalism. This type of donor thinks he knows best how to address other people's needs. The money is used as an instrument for control. In this system, he tends to dictate terms rather than dialogue over the best ways forward.

Some donors have perhaps unconsciously used money to impose their own personal or Western cultural values on a ministry project. That is, their money came with some sharply defined but inappropriate strings attached. Examples of this might be the donor dictating how people were to be trained, how ministry was communicated, what language was used, how stringently financial reporting was done or how the money was divided up. These kinds of things are not bad per se, but if they impose a value system that doesn't fit with local cultural values, then it can do more harm than good. Please don't misunderstand. A weakness of the emerging church in places like Africa and Asia is their lack of planning with clear procedures to accomplish their visionary goals. Nevertheless, a donor with a latent neo-colonialist mentality is usually more interested in instilling his own personal values through his giving than perhaps he is about seeing beneficial impact happen in appropriate ways within the local people's own culture and social system.

Investing in Relationships First

Some donors' common sense business approach to ministry and missions often overlooks the importance of relationship building, which is often considered to be an inefficient and time consuming process. Because these donors are not typically seen as part of the ministry team, they usually lack an easy opportunity to build relations through visits, communications, or other methods and therefore lack the insights into the value of relationships. Consequently, there is no common understanding of what the ministry partners are hoping to achieve together from the start. This sort of mutual understanding is worked out as the project progresses, but by then it is usually too late.

For example, an American church wanted to help an East African church develop a tourism business that could provide funds for the expansion of their mission work in the region. They didn't ask the African church about their business plan or their overhead cost and fee rates because they assumed the church leaders had worked that out. However, when word got back to them that their travel agency was making a significant profit off of American tourists through kickbacks from the motels and touring vehicle companies they arranged, the American church terminated the partnership. In reality, the amount the motels and touring companies were charging the Americans was still rather modest, but it was significantly more than what they charged the less affluent African tourists. The travel agency viewed the money as their commission for using those services, whereas the American church viewed it as a "kickback." Was the African church just behaving shrewdly in generating income the African way?

In general, a weak relationship and lack of pre-existing understanding between both parties results in the donors becoming impatient with a ministry effort. They threaten to cut off funding if progress lags, or they stop funding when they hear of questionable practices by the ministry. Taking the time to establish a closer relationship built on a spirit of collaboration and cultural understanding could result in both parties working through their concerns together to bring about solutions to problems as they inevitably arise. Still, the donors' desire to be fast and efficient in the area of relationships can undermine the results they were hoping to achieve together. Investing in relationships first, either directly, or through a third party, has not always been a priority for some donors.

Withholding Funding

In supporting missions project workers, especially local (i.e. indigenous) workers, some funders provide little to no funding at all. They are the opposite of the type of donor mentioned earlier who believes a lot of money can create success in a ministry endeavor. The non-givers realize how much money has indeed been wasted on poorly planned ministry efforts over the years, with few positive results to show for it. They understand that pouring money into a missionary project doesn't necessarily help the local people who are meant to benefit from the project. Even so, these are less typical reasons why certain people choose not to give to the majority world church and their workers at all. A common reason for not giving is because they do not want to create a dependency on Western funding. How did this paradigmatic thinking come about?

One cultural value that might be behind this fear of creating financial dependency is the "Three-self Paradigm," described as *self-governing, self-supporting* and *self-propagating*. This widely adopted paradigm was popularized by John L. Nevius (1829–1893), an American missionary to China and Korea (Rowell 2006). In relation to the "self-supporting" clause, he feared Western funding for newly planted churches could create an unhealthy dependency on the donors to provide for their ongoing financial needs. Perhaps the Western value of individualism influenced the idea that each new church should work independently by generating its own financial resources to sustain its work. The key word is "sustain." How well have majority world churches sustained their ministry work, let alone expanded it based on this ideal? Hindsight shows that few majority world churches and ministries have ever achieved enough financial independence to greatly expand their work to the degree that Western mission has expected them to. Sustaining the work has suffered from lack of funds. Western missionaries, however, have been typically well-funded in comparison to their national church partners, although they haven't always felt well-funded in their own circumstances.

From Dependency to Mutuality

The shift from concerns about creating financial dependency to greater focus on mutuality in missions is an important topic these days. With the globalization of mission and the socialization of relief efforts, donors and their funding recipient partners need to discuss this topic to avoid some of the pitfalls. Then they can make informed decisions on the effective and non-harmful use of funding.

Partnership is a repeated theme in this book. Yet there are authors who suggest that any financial partnership between a Western donor and a foreign recipient is colonialism and creates dependency. One author declares that interdependency can't be achieved either, and that equality only seems to mean equality in finances (Reese 2010, 67). Granted, mission agencies have made plenty of mistakes over the use of money in their foreign mission work. Even so, the globalized period requires a fresh discussion of the role of money and the people who give it. The opinions of leaders in India and Africa, for example, are needed. In one recent survey, Indian church planters expressed how they still need Western partnership in funding to achieve their visionary goals.[13] How, then, should Western donors and foreign recipients work together?

Two articles on the dependency debate appeared in *Evangelical Missions Quarterly* (Rickett 2012a and 2012b). The books critiqued by the author, Daniel Rickett, are Glenn Schwartz, *When Charity Destroys Dignity* (2007), and John Rowell, *To Give or Not to Give?* (2006). The two authors hold divergent views of money and dependency.

Rickett highlights Schwartz's classic Western mission notion of self-sufficiency. As previously mentioned, this became widely known as part of the three-self paradigm, described as *self-governing, self-supporting,* and *self-propagating.* Rickett states that Schwartz does not actually define dependency. Rather, he describes the unhealthy symptoms of dependency. Many of those symptoms, as Schwartz's book title reveals, have to do with human dignity. He also seeks to avoid inducing cultural conflicts. Some of Schwartz's examples given by Rickett are:

- It tends to erode human dignity.
- It dampens local giving and stifles reliance on God.
- It hinders local initiative.
- It causes jealousy among local Christian leaders who vie for limited Western funds.
- It tends to isolate subsidized pastors from their peers and from systems of local accountability.
- It is often at the root of misappropriated money.

Schwartz believes self-reliance is the solution. The idea "is for local needs to be met with resources that are at hand." He believes interdependence can work only where there is relative equality. That is, where people are "subject to the same economic conditions." In other words, it would be the exception rather than the norm.

---

13 Personal conversation with Steve Roa (2012) on financial partnership in India based on the interviews posted at http://movingmissions.org/outside-funding-of-missions.

John Rowell, on the other hand, according to Rickett, argues that dependency is not as much a problem for indigenous people as it is a problem with North American complacency. He believes the lack of generosity in giving for advancing the gospel is the biggest problem. Western donors should practice a biblical view of wealth and poverty by focusing on maximizing giving, instead of minimizing it, or worse, withholding it for fear of creating dependency.

Rickett provides Rowell's definition of sustainability. Traditionally, the concept was more closely associated with ability to maintain financial resources independent of foreign aid. The ministry should be able to accomplish their projects with the resources at hand, as Schwartz asserts. However, Rowell thinks about sustainability in terms of "sustainable impact." That is, the non-monetary outcomes should be in focus. If the focus is on money rather than results, then all sorts of dysfunctional behavior can occur.

Rickett points out that Schwartz and Rowell agree on some things. For example, outside funds should not limit local leaders' freedom to act on their own vision. Needs should indeed start locally, but Rowell believes that local funding also needs to reach out to provide for what is lacking; otherwise the lack may inhibit sustainable impact. Both agree that money is not the solution. It is just an input. Healthy partnerships are those where everyone contributes meaningfully to the project.

Rickett's solution is interdependency. His own comments seem to support Rowell more than Schwartz, but he does acknowledge some of the problems that Schwartz believes are caused by dependency on Western funding. He believes interdependency is the way to work now in the globalized period.

Here is his seven-point proposal for how the majority world church and the Western church (and donors) could work together more effectively:

1. Eliminate double standards
2. Know the difference between healthy and unhealthy dependency
3. Embrace the responsibilities of wealth
4. Practice development, not betterment

5. Build covenant relationships
6. Facilitate fiscal integrity
7. Pursue sustainable impact

Schwartz's arguments about harm created by outside funding are real, but the solution to not fund at all reveals a degree of Western paternalism. It sounds like Schwartz believes Western donor money causes all sorts of local cultural problems, and not the people using the funds. He seems to assume that indigenous people are not capable of working out those problems, possibly by changing things in their culture that need to change. Is simply withholding the candy, metaphorically speaking, a solution to avoiding tooth decay?

Rickett's discussion of Schwartz and Rowell doesn't cover the globalized period of mission and Christianity which requires major adjustments and new ways of thinking and working. Rowell touches on this period, but he seems to assume traditional Western development principles. Both Schwartz and Rowell appear to have a distinctly Western understanding of biblical stewardship, but one wonders how the recipients of ministry and social service efforts would apply their own understanding of biblical stewardship within their own cultural setting.

Providing funding for all the financial needs of a church could indeed create some forms of dependency, and not helping at all only stifles the work. These days, donors are taking a more balanced approach to this historical Western notion of self-sufficiency by augmenting what is lacking.

A global church discussion is beginning to focus more on resource sharing, and the operating word is "mutuality." Former bishop Hwa Yung addressed this topic well when he said:

> To address adequately the issue of partnership would require us to seriously deal with a whole range of questions. For example, in terms of finance and trained personnel, how and what can the West contribute to augment the meager resources of many non-Western churches? At the same time, how can this be done without giving rise to a dependency mentality on the one hand, and the perpetuation of missionary control on the other? With respect to developing

leadership for non-Western churches up to the highest levels, what can we learn from John Stott's work through the Langham Trust of training national scholars with PhDs? And would international agencies, traditionally under Western control, dare to incorporate non-westerners fully into their leadership on the basis of genuine mutuality? (Yung 2004)

How would Yung's ideas apply in project planning? Before outside funding is decided upon for a project, it is best that the affected community determine what they are capable of contributing. It is safe to assume that God has equipped every community with a variety of gifts, abilities, and resources that can benefit their project.[14] Gift-in-kind services are common ways to assist, but donors and ministry workers should not assume the people with whom they serve are unable or unwilling to provide some financial assistance as well. Then donors can augment what the community is unable to provide on their own. Outside funding is typically needed for things such as full time wages for key workers, training, equipment, and travel cost. This practice seems more aligned with the Apostle Paul's instructions to the Corinthian Christians. A reading of the texts suggests that he did not tell them to provide for all of the needs of people who had less so that they could all be equal in wealth status. He said that everyone should give according to their ability so that all of the people would have what they needed when they needed it.[15]

This kind of financial assistance focuses on the dignity of the local community first, and indeed the community should stretch themselves in the area of faith and funding for their own projects. They might be surprised over what they can accomplish when they realize what God has already provided. Outside funding partners enable the projects to progress well and achieve the effects the ministry work is meant to achieve, with an ability to expand the work for even greater outcomes and sustainable impact.

---

14 See Corbett and Fikkert 2009. The authors make a good case for this.

15 Second Corinthians 8:15. Some readers interpret this as equality of wealth in the sense of socialism. Others read it as everyone helping ensure nobody lacks what they need when they need it.

3

A NEW RELATIONSHIP: WAYS FORWARD

Meet the Church's New Philanthropist: The Twenty-first-century Donor
Are today's pressing social problems less problematic than they were during previous times? Recall the appalling living conditions for so many people in nineteenth century London, Dublin, and New York, the pandemics that killed millions, the inaccessibility to education, and the massive famines that regularly struck parts of Asia and Africa, among other places. Many of these situations improved dramatically over the years with the help of people like Arthur Guinness, Dale Carnegie, and John D. Rockefeller, along with other, more recent action-oriented people, such as World Vision founder Bob Pierce.

During the last sixty years, Western evangelical missions generally avoided working with donors who were interested in alleviating physical suffering and addressing unjust social structures, because those activities could distract the missionaries from what they saw as the more important work of spreading the gospel to new places and making disciples. It's not that they didn't care about people's physical and social needs; they just regarded disease and hunger as a physical problem and injustice as a political issue, whereas bringing gospel enlightenment to the unsaved was a spiritual challenge that needed a separate solution. This was a natural result of their Western (i.e., Greek) dualism that separated things into clean categories, and it is arguable that many Western missionaries brought this mindset to the people they intended to help. However, the people naturally understood that physical and political problems were often the result of spiritual problems, so to address one without the other was less than empowering.

Given so many pressing needs in the twenty-first century (loss of land, human trafficking, drug addiction, social disintegration, HIV/AIDS, war-related trauma), how then should a mission or ministry worker view the church's emerging donors of the twenty-first century? If they are seen as the kinds of people God has raised up over the centuries for the purpose of action, then it falls to ministry leaders to understand what motivates them today, especially if the leaders hope to receive their funding help for their ministries.

Knowing the Emerging Donor: Twelve Characteristics

There are at least two types of new emerging donor. The first type could be called a "renewed giver." They have changed their giving strategies because they think previous strategies are no longer effective. These would be middle-aged or older givers. The second type is the younger giver who may hold to some different values compared to those of the older renewed giver.

CARE ABOUT SUFFERING AND INJUSTICE

Early indicators reveal that the emerging donors, both young and older, but especially the younger ones, still care much about the things Arthur Guinness cared about—alleviating suffering and addressing injustice—and they desire to find accelerated ways to deal with these sorts of problems. However, they desire a more balanced strategy through a holistic approach to human development, one that seeks to address spiritual impoverishment in order to alleviate other kinds of impoverishment, and this is a great encouragement to the people they seek to help. They know a holistic approach is more viable now because of the shift to broader partnership alliances in development projects. Will Western evangelical missions be willing to shift to a more balanced strategy in addressing pressing social issues while planting churches, making disciples, and translating the Bible? Today's donors expect this balance, perhaps more than at any time in the past.

EAGER FOR RAPID CHANGE

Acceleration in problem solving is key because the age of the Internet vastly accelerated the new donor's own ability to gather information rapidly for the purpose of action. This change in technology and information access has also led to greater collaboration, expanding the pool of thinkers and potentially producing results sooner, so donors expect to see this sort of speed in their philanthropic efforts, too.

They also made their money faster, compared to previous times when most philanthropists inherited their wealth.[16] This means the new donors are less interested in building a family legacy than they are in seeing their giving have greater impact. Moreover, much of their wealth was generated by new ideas that took hold, so they naturally seek involvement in projects that apply new, innovative ways of doing things. They are not interested in an agency's traditions or status quo thinking if those things prevent the development of creative solutions to today's problems.

PARTNERSHIP-ORIENTED

Partnership does not suggest equality, unless one thinks of it as "equally capable of contributing something." Additionally, partnership expresses interdependency, especially in a cause-oriented partnership. This means, the cause will not likely succeed unless each partner brings their part to the table. Any significant gap can jeopardize the whole enterprise. In this sense, there is equality in partnership.

As discussed earlier in this book, the most creative and innovative mission agencies began as grassroots partnerships initiated by philanthropists and the laity—the volunteer missionaries. Even so, by the late twentieth century, inter-agency cooperation was no longer a value, ironically even with parachurch organizations. By this time, most countries were neatly divided into regions where only one denominational mission worked, and the notion of working with other agencies through partnership in the same region was not normally considered for fear of "sheep stealing." Instead, a significant concern for mission leaders was guarding their agency's stake in the country.

---

16 The first Arthur Guinness and John D. Rockefeller are notable exceptions.

These days in the social and religious sector, it is unusual to find one entity (church, parachurch, NGO) that is able to implement let alone maintain all critical activities needed to achieve sustainable impact. Now there are calls for the social and religious sectors to seek greater partnership coordination in project planning and implementation. This is for the simple reason that partnership alliances can mobilize more resources and ultimately achieve greater sustainable impact (Wei-Skillern et al. 2007). In evidence of this trend, donors are increasingly requiring partnering as a condition for funding, and in fact, it is often the first thing they look for in a funding proposal.

ASSUME OPEN COLLABORATION

Because twenty-first-century technology allows more people to do things they could never to do before, advancements in internet, phone, and computer technology provide new ways of working together. These vastly improved tools now enable more people and organizations to network on a greater scale, to build partnership alliances, to freely share their ideas and experiences and seek to apply better practices in any ministry effort. The new donors want to partner with organizations that are transparent for the sake of effective collaboration, and they use these tools to allow that collaboration to grow. Indeed, the new donors desire direct interaction with project leaders on the ground, because they view direct partnership as a dynamic part of their role in the ministry effort.

DOERS—NOT JUST GIVERS

The new donors see giving as an investment and not a gift, so pandering and flattery won't convince them to give more, if it ever did. Instead, a clear vision with a well-thought-out plan is more compelling. Yet, clinging to the belief that donors are only interested in giving would be a mistake. A significant difference with many of today's donors is that they want to invest money in missions and ministries, but they also want to invest their time and their ideas.[17] Many of them are creative thinkers who go against

---

17 The rate of high net worth people volunteering more than two hundred hours per year increased from 26.7 percent in 2007 to 39.3 percent in 2009 (Osili et al. 2010, 51).

conventional wisdom, and that can be unsettling for a funding recipient. Yet, organizations that seek the former without considering the latter will probably not see the donor's lasting involvement with their ministry. Including them as full partners in appropriate ways is one way to show genuine respect for the donor's talents and experiences, too.

In fact, an organization's traditional understanding of legacy and branding is no longer keeping donors engaged, as perhaps those things did in the past. There has been a steady decline in the number of people (typically donors and volunteers in the social sector) visiting an organization's official website and an increase in visiting an organization's social branding community. That is, an organization's legacy and brand is still important, but what is drawing donors more and more is the opportunity to help shape programs through a social network rather than an official website, which treats visitors more like consumers. This is another indication that givers desire to be involved in causes in greater ways.

RISK TAKERS AND EXPERIMENTERS

In the era of global giving, risk comes with the territory. Seth Godin said, "The safer you play your plans for the future, the riskier it actually is. That's because the world is certainly, definitely, and more than possibly changing" (Godin 2008). The new donors understand this, because they were not risk averse in their own careers. They know that if you are not failing at anything, then you are not trying anything new, because with experimentation comes occasional failure, and that is okay with them. Indeed, they are not intimidated by obstacles or problems as long as project leaders have a plan to overcome them.

A new trend in the business and social sector is crowdsourcing (Surowiecki 2005). This notion is based on the theory that aggregating more diverse knowledge, skills, wisdom, experience, and insights in an endeavor can produce much better results. This is in comparison to what can be produced by a closed group of only a few experts. Now, some mission agencies are beginning to apply this notion to localize everything from training curriculum development to Scripture translation. But it does involve risk. Opening up important mission endeavors to the affected masses means giving up certain areas of control. The upside is that it can produce greater community involvement, which generates pride of ownership with increased quality and greater outcomes. People don't know until they try something new, and then the results, while imperfect, might surprise them. The new emerging donors are willing to take such risks if the results can propel a ministry's work into the future for greater results.[18]

Even so, many ministries view experimentation on the mission field as too risky and too time consuming, hence not a good use of funds. For example, one consulting company suggested that an indicator of a mission agency's good use of money was the amount of donor funds sent directly to their field to sustain current work, and sending 90 percent rates a high score. Sending more money to where it matters most is certainly a good thing, but this company is telling their clients to be risk averse. They do not understand that a percentage of operating funds should be put toward experimentation at the field level, where greater impact is desired. An overly cautious approach is to only fund what is known and currently working. But what is currently working may not work so well in the future, and without experimentation to discover new ways of working, nothing will be in place when the tried and true ways have lost their optimal usefulness. Saving money by avoiding experimentation will actually result in greater cost later on.

One organization that has had success in taking programs to scale internationally put it this way:

> In most public or nonprofit service organizations, innovation is seen as a luxury, not a necessity. So it does not receive the sustained investment, management, and talent development that it requires . . . For us, investment in the process of innovation itself provided the crucial breakthrough. (Stone 2001, 45)

Lately, more donors assume an "appropriate" amount of spending on overhead for experimentation and innovation, but what is considered

---

18 Recent study indicates that 54 percent of high net worth donors are willing to take average risk, whereas 31 percent are willing to take above average risk, and nearly 5 percent would take substantial risk (ibid.,67).

appropriate varies. One author commented that only allowing a small overhead has harmed the work of non-profits for years because they haven't had the financial space to experiment where their mission impact takes place (Park 2001). These days, donors are increasingly aligning with thoughtful experimenters, especially if it means increasing an organization's efficiency and effectiveness to create greater benefit for the people they serve. They understand that some iterative experimentation for innovation is a good use of the funds they give, too. The authors of *The Other Side of Innovation* recommend earlier innovative experiments be cheap and iterative for the purpose of learning (Govindarajan and Trimble 2010).

RE-INVENTORS

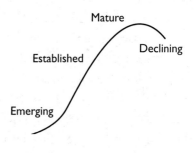

Effectiveness Curve

As noted in the previous section, smart business leaders know that specific ways of doing things have a limited life span. Some people view such a life span following an s-curve, as illustrated here. At first new ideas, methods, or processes create a surge in effectiveness because they are well-aligned with the times. However, as time goes on, methods become less effective because the world has changed. These days, the new donors, especially young entrepreneurs, assume missions should also undergo re-engineering every so often to realign with the times. They look for ministries that are willing to periodically reconsider practices so that mission effectiveness does not decline over time. A typical business cycle s-curve is about five years, and some mission agencies have effectively used this analytical planning tool and time frame to keep pace with rapid change in the world. A ministry's unwillingness to deal with poor or declining performance makes them far less attractive to donors. Today, willingness to change is valued over the more traditional values of consistency and stability.

WELL-INFORMED

At one time, donors relied on mission leaders to inform them about the physical and spiritual needs of the people the mission was serving. However, today the average donor is far more informed on needs in the world thanks to an abundance of information sources, most notably by means of Google and other internet search tools. Surveys also indicate that the new donors are more highly educated than the general US public in that 54 percent have completed a four-year degree, compared to the general population figure of 27 percent (McLeish 2007).

Even obscure knowledge can surface. One donor learned that a project he considered funding was located on an island in the Pacific that was sinking, and that made him wonder how much longer the people would remain on the island. It turns out the island wasn't sinking all that fast. Still, quick internet research provided him with information the mission agency was not aware of. What other bits of information do donors have when funding appeals are made?

In order to provide better due diligence with funding proposals, it's not unusual for a large foundation to have their own research department, so it should be no surprise to discover just how well-informed potential donors can be. New consulting companies continue to emerge and provide rigorous due diligence for donors that don't have research departments, so now even these donors expect ministries and mission agencies to demonstrate, in compelling ways, that they have an up-to-the-minute understanding of circumstances, needs, challenges, and leveraging options. Agencies that are unprepared with this sort of information will cause serious concern. The new donors desire to partner with agencies that have done their homework, because so many of them have done theirs.

CAUSE-ORIENTED

In earlier times, missionary projects often focused on narrowly defined religious settings, such as animist, Muslim, and Hindu groups, or on broad "ethnic" groups, such as Nigerian and Pacific Islander, and so on. Campaigns to spread the gospel to specific religions and cultures generated vaguely defined terms, such as "people groups," which spawned narrower terms like "unreached people groups," and then the more specific "unreached and unengaged people groups." Fund-raising campaigns invited Western donors to adopt a people group. Although these descriptions, especially the adoption concept, now sound a bit paternalistic, the heart motive behind the terminology was genuine; there were entire groups of people and cultures that had never heard the gospel. Nevertheless, many of today's donors desire to participate in even more narrowly defined causes that seek solutions to problems faced by individual people and entire people groups in holistic ways. Being cause-oriented requires viewing physical and spiritual problems as a tightly interwoven reality rather than separate problems that require separate solutions, hence the donor's desire to focus on causes that bring relief to pressing physical, spiritual, and cultural problems. The results of these more focused causes can spread through an entire group of people and their culture, thus bringing change on a large scale in the long run.

OUTCOME- AND IMPACT-ORIENTED

The new donors do not view a ministry's activities or their outputs (i.e., things they produce) as end goals per se. Rather, they see those things as necessary steps to achieve impact in people's lives; impact that is meaningful and measureable. Indeed, they assume that whatever a ministry does, there is measurability so that all partners know how well they are doing in creating positive change. One venture philanthropy firm asserts that "assessment and managing to outcomes will become more widespread in the future. Eventually, this discipline will become the norm" (Morino 2011, loc. 279–96).

A ministry's measurement methods may include the use of statistics, but these days donors are less trusting of purely statistical reports that paint rosy pictures or present dire needs. Plus, counting alone can't confirm intangible things like spiritual transformation. Therefore, they also want stories from people served by the ministry, the kinds of stories that reveal deep-level transformation in their life and the life of their community. Impact may come in a variety of forms, so ministry leaders need to know what those forms are to figure out how to measure them. The donors also look for measurements that reveal significant advances, such as growth in organizational capacity, leadership, and partnership alliances.

Donors also want to hear the full story, the problems and failures the ministry projects have encountered along the way, because those are also important factors to monitor. In fact, they look on impact reports that only focus on positive outcomes with suspicion, because they know that in the real world things rarely go perfectly according to plan.

LONG-TERM-ORIENTED

Short-term impatience and a desire for greater results do not mean the new donors are uninterested in long-term effects. For example, they are less interested in partnering with ministries that do things for people rather than with people, because the former way is not a sustainable model. In other words, a ministry's measurement of success and greatness has much to do with how much capacity is developed among the people they serve. Are they helping to equip the people with skills to sustain the work long after the partnership engagement is over, or are they only using the people as a means to their own ends? Are they creating incentives for people to follow through on their roles? Are they assisting people with their own organizational development, or are they only maintaining their own organizational presence? Investing in capacity building increases long-term effects. The new donors know this, so they are willing to commit long-term funding for that reason.

ABHORRENCE OF WASTE

The new donors may not live as frugally as previous generations, but this does not mean they are tolerant of poor use of funds. Some of them question the large amount of money spent supporting foreign missionaries over the years and wonder how much was achieved given the financial cost. Now more donors are bypassing missionaries to give directly to national and indigenous ministry workers. They are doing this because of the workers' broad experience and ability to carry out quality projects through partnership and at a significantly lower cost. This means Western ministries now need to justify the cost of their projects in ways they didn't have to in the past. Even so, funding recipients should not assume the new donor is only interested in "cheap." They know that underfunded projects can progress slowly and perform poorly, so developing optimal budgets that show clear and effective use of funding has greater credibility in their eyes.

In summary, all of these characteristics fall under the rubric of strategic thinking. That is, to produce maximum beneficial impact, planning requires the aggregation of several things, such as a clearly stated vision and a well-defined mission governed by shared values, with clear steps to guide the process through to completion. It requires learning through experimentation to avoid stagnation. Periodic reinvention is needed when the status quo is no longer achieving an acceptable level of mission impact. These are the sorts of things today's emerging donors look for in a ministry or mission agency's project planning and practices.

On the surface, some ministries may appear to have well-thought-out strategic plans in place, while in fact there is a large gap between rhetoric and reality in their plans. That means they have a compelling mission statement, high quality brochures and websites, and skilled fundraising professionals, but if you dig deeper, you discover that their strategic thinking is rather shallow. They have vision and a desire to make a meaningful impact in their area of ministry, but with a lack of sound research and clear planning, the results may be limited in comparison to the human and financial cost of their work.

Make no mistake about it: this sort of strategic thinking in mission is missiological thinking, even if the language of missiology is not used. The primary goal of missiology is to figure out the most effective ways to participate in God's mission of communicating the gospel in local cultural and religious context. In the past, sound business practices were not normally included in missiological thinking because of missionary bias against business in general, as well as the division between the laity (the business person/funder) and the ministry (the minister and missionary). Today, however, it is more common to integrate this sort of strategic thinking in culturally sensitive and respectful ways, thus filling a gap that has existed in missiological thinking over the last several decades.

Increasingly, today's donors are taking a closer look at all of the areas mentioned in this section, as they should be. Is it possible that God is working through people like them to help improve ministry and mission effectiveness for the sake of the gospel during these globalizing and fast-paced times?

Renewal of the Donor-Recipient Relationship

It's time to hit the reset button on the donor-recipient relationship in missions and ministry in general. The first thing ministries need to do is eject the unbiblical notion of a hierarchical division of labor between the ministry and the laity. Whether a person is seminary-educated or business school–educated, there is only one ministry, and God spreads his ministerial gifts generously to everyone who calls themselves a follower of Jesus. Each person is both leader and follower in his or her ministry.

Next, they need to change the way they talk about ministry partnership. When discussing ministry partnership models, a term Western partners commonly use is "stakeholder." In the business sector, it means having an interest in a project or a business enterprise, and the stakeholder needs to guard the value to avoid loss. A mission agency's stake could be money, leadership, or even ways of doing things. A negative view of this borrowed business term is that stakeholders are usually more concerned about guarding their own interest than they are in investing to create value in others involved in the project and thus creating more value for the whole. This mentality can negatively influence the entire project, especially if each partner has the same attitude. This is "stakeholderism," and it is particularly prevalent in Western mission work.

Profile of a Twenty-first-century Giver

Paul is a young director of a well-endowed foundation. He believes that effective philanthropy should be holistic; in other words, it should consider all forms of impoverishment—inclusive of the spiritual, physical, relational, and environmental. He believes interactions with grantees should not be transactional but relational. Philanthropists like Paul don't want grantees to be afraid to tell the foundation about their real problems; they desire transparency. They want to work in partnership with local leaders, to know the root causes of the problems in order to help create a more sustainable solution.

This does not mean partners should be careless about their wise use of money, time, or personnel in a collaborative effort. What it does mean is that the partners should view themselves as co-ministers who exist for one another to accomplish something bigger than the individual parts. Rather than each partner guarding over their individual contribution, they focus on how their contribution can enhance the work as a whole. Each partner brings something for the benefit of the others rather than just for themselves.

Stakeholderism means that a mission agency views their role as simply bringing something to the mission effort. It's a one-way view of ministry, because reciprocal learning from the people they serve is not usually part of their plan. They hold strongly to the things they bring. They are emotionally attached to those things, because it is their "stake" in the work. As a result, they are unwilling to think about shifting to a reciprocal model, one that could produce better results in the long term.

An example of guarding a stake may be short-term volunteer builders insisting on doing the construction work themselves because they think they can do a better job. A reciprocal approach would be builders willing to learn from and train locals to produce quality environment-appropriate structures for themselves. For another example, a training organization may insist on "bringing" training methods and a curriculum that they have always used. A reciprocal approach would be working with the people they serve to determine the best training methods and most appropriate curriculum based on mutual learning.

To know if you are practicing stakeholderism, ask yourself, "Is my contribution a one-way activity? Will it create the kind of value that can enhance the success of other partners in the project, or is it mostly just

ensuring that I am able to do something that has greater personal value
to me?"

What Drives All Partners?

These days, what drives all partners most is seeing meaning and hope
in what they do. For the donors, giving is a way to satisfy their desire
to help create positive change in a dysfunctional world. They also desire
to freely associate with like-minded people who share their passion,
regardless of official position or rank in mission and ministry. It's not
like this notion of free and equal association in ministry on the part of
the donor has been entirely lost, but as I have attempted to explain thus
far, it has become the exception rather than the norm that it once was.
Writing in 1837, one American mission thinker pointed out how "it is the
contributors of the funds who are the real association . . . the individuals,
churches, congregation, who freely act together, through such agencies
for an object of common interest. The Protestant form of free, open,
responsible, embracing all classes, both sexes, all ages, the masses of the
people, is peculiar to modern times, almost to our age." Significantly, this
person observed that this movement was a reappearance from an earlier
time in Christian history (Walls 1988, 141–155). Could it be that now in
the twenty-first century, yet another appearance of these earlier times in
Christian history is occurring, when ministry is viewed as the work of all
people regardless of their official standing in the church?

Rather than repeating ministry's hubris of earlier times by assuming
naiveté at best or selfish intentions at worst on the part of the donor,
ministry workers need to discover what is actually in the donor's heart.
With a renewed partnership model, the donor is on equal standing with
mission and ministry workers. Both the donor and the worker influence
one another, as is always the case in true partnership. Each brings their
God-entrusted spiritual gifts to bear in the collaborative effort. Each
contributes solutions to improve the partnership. Any arrogance or
mistrust on the part of the ministry concerning donors (individuals and
foundations) needs to be replaced with appreciation for the financial
provision the donors are tasked by God to provide for the ministry.

Indeed, if the donors truly understand the serious responsibility God has placed on their shoulders for the greater good of the project, then they will work hard to ensure that their participation is actually adding value to the effort as a whole and that they are not practicing stakeholderism with their money.

A collaborative effort is important from the start in project planning. In a sense, developing partnership collaboration is like building a covenant community. Rather than suggesting that we begin by stating our personal positions and "stakes" in the project, Fuller Theological Seminary professor of anthropology Sherwood Lingenfelter offers a different procedure. First, he suggests starting with worship. The partners' attitude should be that of collective worship, but not in the sense of gathering together, holding hands, and singing worship songs, especially where widely divergent languages and worship styles converge. He means the collective attitude of the heart. With this form of corporate worship, our service in the partnership is sacrifice—our bodies, possessions, praise, and often our personal preferences. Then he suggests having an attitude of mutual learning. That is, reflecting on the cultural assumptions each partner brings to the effort. It means awareness of how one behaves in their culture and how that behavior affects the community. To work as part of a covenant community, each participant needs to think about how to adjust their practices in ways that can enhance the collaboration. That does not mean devaluing one's own cultural norms and values but placing those on the altar of worship, especially if holding on to certain practices is detrimental to what the community hopes to accomplish. It replaces self-interest with group-interests (Lingenfelter 2008, 81–90).

Understanding Your Partner's Ministry Language

Donors, especially major givers, generally come from a business culture. They speak the language of business and they assume that people they partner with understand what they consider to be standard language. When they question a funding recipient, they might use terms such as "rate of return," "measurements," and "benchmarks." Nevertheless, this language has been objectionable for many of the faith-based generation of missionaries, that is, people who believed that business practices in mission work and fundraising were not part of faith-based living. Because of this bias against business practices in ministry, which they often confused with the negative effects of capitalistic practices (see "The Emergence of Donor-driven Planning" in chapter 1), the faith-based generation avoided using business language to discuss ministry planning. Anything business-sounding was suspicious.

This language bias is an unmistakable mark of ministers and missionaries of this generation, whether they realize it or not. So what language do they use? They might respond to the donor's questions with rather abstract spiritual jargon, such as "redemptive analogies," "incarnational ministry," and "church planting movements." They might even use an occasional abstruse phrase like "theological imperative," as already used by this author! They insist that good things are happening with their ministry, but they have an aversion to developing sound metrics to validate their claims. Their language does not engender confidence with the donor, because it all sounds so otherworldly.

With the covenant community partnership model, both the donor and the recipient need to recognize the limitations of their own understanding and seek to understand the "meaning" behind the language of the other rather than feeling offended by it on the one hand or assuming naiveté on the other.

What follows is a quick reference tool to help the spiritually abstract-minded ministry worker understand the language of the business-minded donor. This list of terms and definitions shows what most donors are thinking when they use business language. They want the same things the ministry workers want: good outcomes, positive change, good use of resources, and integrity in doing what the ministry claimed it would do. Still, donors should not assume that everybody speaks or at least understands their language, and that is okay. Many people in ministry have good business minds even if they don't use the lingo, so donors also need to seek understanding of the meaning behind the ministry language the workers use.

Figure 1. Understanding Your Partner's Language

Donor Language	Ministry Worker Interpretation
Investment	What you are sacrificially providing to launch and grow the ministry effort
Business Model	Steps to accomplish your visionary goals
Performance	How progress is made to accomplish the goals
Return on Investment (ROI)	Good effects of the project based on what it cost to achieve it
Measurement Metrics	The sorts of things that confirm the mission goals are being achieved
Scorecard	Comparison of a mission statement to what is actually being accomplished by the mission work
Annual Yield	Good results over the year

This is what mutual learning in a covenant community is about. It's putting our preferential language and comfort zone on the altar of worship by making an effort to understand the other person's language and cultural perspective. This way, the partners fill each other's knowledge gaps, as opposed to one partner having to learn the ministry language and culture of the other with no humble reciprocal learning in return.

Preferential or Deferential Treatment?

It is nice to receive preferential treatment. Frequent fliers discover the benefits of status when the airline upgrades them to the first class cabin, and they even get to board the plane first! It's quite intoxicating.

God's word says believers, as the church, are not to treat people preferentially based on wealth, social status, or any other determining factor that favors one person over the other.[19] This scriptural principle is cited by some ministry and mission leaders as the reason they do not give donors special treatment. Among other things, it means they don't invite the donors to give feedback on their project spending, nor do they provide more explanations and better quality reporting just because

---

19 James 2:1–2 and Mark 10:35–41, for examples.

these people give more money than the average person. That would be showing favoritism, according to them. Chapter 2 of James' Epistle is most commonly quoted in reference to this, and the examples given by James do indeed describe the sort of preferential treatment people are to avoid. However, applying James' teaching so broadly with respect to the role of major financial givers goes beyond what he taught.

People on ministry teams typically treat one another with deference. That is, they show courteous respect and regard for the role that each person plays on the team. They cooperate with one another for the sake of the work, and they acknowledge the importance of each person's role in public gatherings. In line with biblical teaching, regular church members are supposed to honor their spiritual leaders too, because people who carry extra responsibilities within the church are indeed deserving of deferential treatment.[20] Yet, when it comes to finances, it seems ministry leaders have been less willing to show deference in tangible ways to those who are called to give generously to church and ministry. Exceptions to this can be found with parachurch organizations, but it is generally true with churches and denomination mission agencies. However, if ministry workers view major givers as people God has tasked to carry a greater weight of responsibility in the area of finances, then they should be willing to defer to them in accordance with that role the same way they defer to pastors, Bible teachers, or missionaries for their service.

Showing respect to a major giver does not mean boasting about their level of giving, nor does it necessarily mean attaching their names in public ways to certain projects. Many donors would rather keep their level of giving confidential, and that is okay. Instead, it means offering to include them on project planning and spending discussions. It also means providing good quality reports on project progress and outcomes so they feel reassured over the effective use of the money. This shows they are valued for more than just their money, and it acknowledges that generous givers are part of the ministry team, as Paul's teaching in Romans 12:8 describes it.

---

20 I Thessalonians 5:12.

Mutual Accountability in Ministry

With the church, few people would question the notion that they are accountable to one another. This recurring New Testament theme is meant to produce spiritually healthy individuals, and it benefits the church as a whole. Yet it seems this notion of mutual accountability has been applied in limited ways in ministry projects. It may be because of the stark division of labor between the doers (the ministers and missionaries) and the supporters (the funders) that developed over time. Each person is expected to faithfully carry out their role for the work to progress. You do your part, and I'll do mine. That seems to be the extent of the accountability relationship, and it sounds more like a contractual or even a transactional agreement.

I suggest that a biblical model of accountability is not contractual or transactional, but rather mutually beneficial. For a donor, mutual accountability requires humility because it means inviting a ministry partner to freely ask questions, make suggestions, and point out concerns over how the donor applies their funding help. The word "mutual" means bi-directional. The ministry worker needs the donor's feedback, and the donor needs the ministry worker's feedback. This is known as a feedback loop. Business enterprises depend heavily on customer feedback, hence the requests for "a brief survey" that pops up regularly on web pages. A smart company wants to have some reasonable assurance that their customer base is satisfied with their product or service, so they find ways to generate useful feedback from the customers to know how they are doing. Could this notion of customer satisfaction be applied in spiritually apt ways in a donor-recipient partnership?

Imagine a donor (an individual or a foundation) sending a survey questionnaire to a ministry partner asking for their feedback on how they are doing as a funding partner. The survey might contain questions such as "How is our giving enabling you to achieve your mission goals?" "How does our report form assist you in knowing what to report or how to report project outcomes?" "Is the way we fund (annually, quarterly, etc.) helpful or problematic?" "Please suggest how we can improve the way we participate in this project."

Ministry workers need feedback from donors, too. They could ask questions such as "How well does our reporting keep you informed about progress and setbacks in this project?" "Are the ways we report on progress satisfying, or are there other things you'd like know about project outcomes that would be more valuable?" "Do you feel included or excluded from key decisions made during the course of the project?"

Because a partner voluntarily seeks information about their own performance, the questions do not communicate a watchdog mentality, nor do they express a lack of trust. Indeed, mutual feedback loops of this sort are meant to show genuine care and concern for the other partners in the collaboration, and humility is required when the survey answers reveal a weakness or problem with their practices. A feedback loop provides a partner with valuable input that can improve the project in vital ways if the partners are willing to listen. In some cultural settings it will require the help of a third-party participant to collect honest feedback from a partner. The intermediary helps to validate beneficial practices and expose areas of weakness between project partners in less confrontational ways. One author refers to this as "strategy accountability." It is a "proactive approach to addressing concerns that can strengthen trust and confidence by increasing transparency, improving performance, and achieving the stated mission" (Green 2011, 71–82).

Smart companies also regularly conduct internal self-evaluations through the use of a "scorecard." This checklist helps them know how well they are carrying out their strategic plan. Low scores mean poor performance, and so on. In the non-profit world, including missionary work, using a scorecard means honestly assessing how well the ministry is doing the things they told their project partners they would do. Low scores mean the people depending on their role are not served or helped in the way that the ministry said they would. High scores mean they are excelling in their role, and that is helping them to be successful in what they are doing. Scorecards can help both the donors and recipients assess their own performance, i.e., faithfulness and excellence, in the collaborative effort.

Donors who simply hand over their money to mission and ministry with the assumption that those funds will be used well and positive impact will occur are becoming a minority. Increasingly, the new emerging donors view their involvement in much the same way businesses view strategic partnerships. That means factors such as plans, benchmarks, and outcome reporting are worked out jointly by all parties in one way or another before they agree to work together. It is easier to be accountable for our own role in a partnership if this sort of clarity has been worked out between partners from the beginning, and then feedback loops and scorecards help each partner monitor internal and external progress.

Knowing What Success Looks Like

It is hard for a donor or a ministry worker to know how well a collaborative effort is performing if both participants have a different understanding of what success looks like. A donor-recipient relationship over a Bible translation project in India was severely strained because both parties had quite a different view of what success was in that project. The Bible translator was reporting the number of literacy classes he was conducting, the number of people attending prayer services, the number of baptisms occurring, and the language analysis he was doing. To him, these activities were building blocks for a successful translation project, but the donors did not know that. Instead, they were wondering why after three years so little Scripture translation had been completed. That was why they were supporting the project, so in their view the project was not achieving much success.

A donor was giving to a Ghanaian organization to improve the quality of education in rural villages. He assumed donor reports would tell how many Ghanaian school children were advancing to higher grades, but the reports only told about the completion of school building construction, which was an indicator of success for the organization they supported.

Profile of a Twenty-first-century Giver

Fred is the director of a major foundation. The foundation isn't interested in average sorts of projects that follow a predictable approach. Instead, they focus on the more challenging, untraditional kinds of projects that are more difficult to fund. To determine if a project is a good fit for the foundation, Fred wants to know what the ministry leader's vision is and what he expects God to do in the long term through that vision. That means the leader needs to explain in fairly clear terms what success will look like. Then Fred asks them to describe their first steps in launching their visionary effort. In other words, can they show a clear plan to achieve the success they described? Now with a good understanding of the ministry's visionary goals and plans, the foundation is ready to work with them. Fred says that because of this partnership building process, the foundation only asks for an annual report from the funding recipient. If they couldn't trust them over the course of a year, then they probably would not enter into a working relationship with them at all.

In the India and Ghana projects, there was a lack of understanding over what each partner assumed were valid indicators of success. Because today's donors desire to know about benchmarks and success indicators before they give, it is more important than ever for funding recipients to determine clear project outcomes (i.e., what success looks like) and then describe that well in a funding proposal. They also need to determine the sorts of progress indictors they will look for to know how they are doing in moving toward their ultimate aim. Finally, they need to decide on the kinds of incremental benchmarks they will use to know if they are moving towards completion within their proposed timeframe.

This information is vital for any project funding proposal these days, and it is not just meant to satisfy a donor's desire for information. Importantly, it helps the project workers understand what their impact aims are, and secondly, providing this information will educate a potential donor over the sorts of things they should be looking for when they receive progress reports from the workers. This sort of clarity from the start is vital in establishing a mutual understanding of success, and it enables partners to agree over what the project goals are from the very beginning. Donors are certainly willing to take risks when they understand the sort of positive impact risk taking can produce, and this sort of mutual understanding helps to prevent the partnership from collapsing when success does not come as easily as either partner thought it would.

In India, this sort of clarity from the start would have helped donors know the sorts of activities the Bible translator planned to carry out to build a foundation for community acceptance and use of the translated Scriptures, and then the translator's reports would have made more sense to them. In Ghana, the education organization would have first explained to their donors how a quality community-owned and community-built school building would produce a healthier and safer learning environment and that it would also leverage more government help. These important first steps would lead towards improvements in the quality of education in these isolated village settings.

4

THE PARACHURCH IN DECLINE

Money on the Move Again

Is the parachurch of the twentieth century in decline? The missiologist Samuel Escobar thinks it should end, or at least change its ways in order to be effective in the twenty-first century. His primary criticism relates to how modern mission agencies "bypassed their indigenous partners in order to perpetuate their own independence . . . " (Escobar 2003, 68). It does seem to be a general mark of Western mission during this period. This is not so much hindsight criticism. Rather, it is a call to re-evaluate mission agency strategies given the present times. Indeed, there are many donors among the people challenging current practices in both church and missions. They are doing it through their questions, and as in former times, they are also doing it through their giving.

It does appear that the modern parachurch is in decline. And if history is any indicator, this is when donor funding begins to shift to where it will have the greatest effect, so where is it going now? Nowadays, donors are increasingly bypassing Western denominational missions and parachurch ministries to give directly to indigenous ministries in Africa, Asia, Latin America, and the Pacific. They are doing this for some of the same reasons giving shifted from the mainline church to the parachurch sixty years ago. They see more funds used to cover internal operating needs, reduced effectiveness, hubris, and misalignment with the times.

The emergence of mature and strong churches overseas certainly calls into question giving models that developed during the modern parachurch era. As discussed in chapter 1, donor-designated giving became the method of choice because donors generally understood where their funds went and how those funds were used. In addition, the donor-recipient model of the last sixty years is also changing. This is because the model indicates a clear demarcation between roles, leaving donors feeling like they are in a contractual or transactional relationship, and that is not satisfying to them, if it ever was.

Historically, a significant catalyst for the parachurch movement has been the high level of volunteerism, especially during the latter part of the twentieth century. That movement peaked around 1987, and since then the number of young people joining mission agencies and raising their own financial support has been in decline, at least in regard to long-term service. Does the decline indicate that the two-hundred-year-old cross-cultural missionary movement is coming to an end? Given the shift of Christianity to global southern regions, and the shift of donor giving to their indigenous ministries, the answer to this question is probably yes. The parachurch is experiencing rapid decline, and this at a time when ten to forty trillion dollars could pass from the Depression-era generation to the Baby Boomer generation and their children over the next twenty-five years (Bishop and Green 2008, 28).

The Age of Global Giving

Retracing the shift in donor giving first mentioned in chapter 1, the historic giving progression looks like this:

As discussed in chapter 3, these days more donors desire to be viewed as co-laborers—equal partners working together to achieve a common cause. In the past, stewardship was associated with designated giving, and now partnership is associated with direct giving with personal involvement.

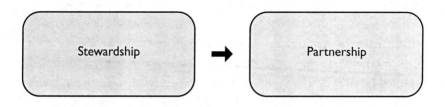

Given these changes, how should parachurch ministries respond? Is there even a need for parachurch mission organizations to exist given the rise of the Global South church? To answer this question, let's recall what the DNA of the parachurch movement has been over the centuries.

Old DNA in New Times

In chapter 1, we saw how the early parachurch was the most creative part of the church. Their DNA comprised philanthropy, entrepreneurship, creativity, boldness, and most of all a bias towards action. Individuals like William Carey, with no official standing in the church, were not afraid to challenge the status quo, and they did it in bold ways at times.[21] The movement manifested itself through volunteerism, creative fundraising, and the formation of missionary societies to send the volunteer workers overseas. By the late twentieth century, parachurch volunteers were better trained and better equipped to work in some of the most challenging places on earth. Ralph Winter said that, even though the ecumenical church viewed them as second-class, "they produced a movement that is impossibly large and robust—and not easy to manage!" (Winter 1992). However, over time their freedom to try new things eroded, and when an organization's creative climate collapses so goes its ability to be flexible and responsive to change.

Assuming the universal church is still gifted with philanthropic, entrepreneurial, and innovative people, what sorts of things might they bring to the work of mission and ministry these days? If the parachurch

---

21 For example, the title of William Carey's 1792 tract, "An Enquiry into the Obligation of Christians to Use Means for the Conversion of the Heathens, in Which the Religious State of the Different Nations of the World, the Success of Former Undertakings, and the Practicality of Further Undertakings, Are Considered."

does undergo reinvention, how will it manifest itself in twenty-first-century mission? Will the mainstream view these people as heretics and write them off as irrelevant, or will they seek ways to freely and openly collaborate with them for the greater good? Will there be mutual respect, viewing one another as equal members of the church, or will they be viewed as amateur players in mission and ministry? These questions still remain to be answered. Yet there are areas where the creative genius of the grassroots church is beginning to bring significant change now in the twenty-first century.

A Glimpse at the New Parachurch

The new parachurch, if that term still applies, is taking on a remarkably different look these days. People shouldn't be surprised over this considering the creative and action-oriented thinking that has characterized the volunteer church over the last two centuries. From the very beginning, people on the margin of mainstream ministry were the most creative and innovative risk takers. Perhaps the notion of "para"—on the fringe—is still where we should expect to find the fresh thinkers of today as well. However, is the new parachurch a reinvention of itself or is it undergoing a rebirthing as something entirely new? Tim Keller thinks it is easier to plant a new church than go through the process of reshaping an old church to be relevant during changing times, because the old church tends to prefer the old ways (Keller 2002). Likewise, is it easier to launch a new parachurch organization than to apply the difficult and disciplined process of reinventing an old organization for the same reasons?

It appears that few established mainline and parachurch mission agencies are applying the rigors of reinvention for the sake of relevancy these days. However, given that relevancy and reinvention are an important value to many donors, how will a lack of willingness to change affect ministry funding over the next decade or so? The following section gives one example of a parachurch organization that is trying to realign with the times. Even so, confirming Keller's opinion, birthing something new rather than retuning something old is how the twenty-first-century parachurch is dealing with change, and with this comes the emergence of new specialty service organizations.

THE TRAINING ORGANIZATION

Believers in global southern regions provide visionary and capable leadership. They are resilient often because of persecution. They desire acceleration because of urgency, so they are looking for new and better ways to work. In regions where the greatest needs are, they desire global partnership for training and equipping ministry workers. Now some parachurch organizations are retooling to provide this sort of help. It is their unique and appropriate contribution to the partnership alliance these days. However, change requires boldness, determination, and discipline for an aging organization to retool for more effective service in new roles. Donors are observing how these old organizations are retooling to see if their action brings new value to partnership alliances these days, and they will invest their money accordingly.

THE RESEARCH ORGANIZATION

A new look coming from the parachurch is the development of non-profit agencies that provide a specialized service. One such service is project planning. As noted earlier in this book, some people object to what they perceive to be a Western management model that is more interested in efficiency and predictability. However, missiologist James Plueddemann notes, "Many practical problems emerging churches face result from a lack of planning and management" (Plueddemann 2006, 256). These new organizations believe there are sound business and organizational practices that are useful in any cultural context. At first, indigenous partners may think these organizations' processes are hierarchical and closed, but over time they realize the systems are necessary in order for them to achieve success in their projects. Even so, adhering rigorously to certain business practices is not the goal of these organizations. Rather they desire to help indigenous ministries develop planning and management practices that enhance their projects and allow them to carry out out their visionary ideas with good results in culturally appropriate ways.

Monitoring and measuring results to know how well a ministry is achieving its strategic goals is an important internal management tool. But those practices are usually lacking in mission and ministry work. Indeed, these days it is also important to provide quality impact reports to donors so they know how their involvement is helping to produce good effects. However, knowing what to measure and how to measure can be challenging for ministries, and the donors may not know what valid indicators of success are. To help meet these needs, new non-profit organizations like Metadigm Group, Calvin Edwards & Company, Global Scripture Impact, and Global Mapping International have formed to provide this sort of specialized service for ministries and donors. Like other alliance partners, these organizations care about what the ministries care about: having the best possible effect on the people the ministry serves.

THE RESOURCING ORGANIZATION

Simply stated, the globalization of mission and ministry means that more people in more places are launching more ministry efforts in more creative ways than ever before. Indeed, entrepreneurship in the social and religious sector is a result of volunteerism, because people need worthy causes to give their lives meaning. It is not unusual for even the wealthiest of philanthropists to admit that solving social problems with their wealth is more rewarding to them than the making of their wealth. It's well-documented that people who volunteer for a cause are happier and even physically healthier than people who don't (Brooks 2002, 138). However, as in the earliest days of the parachurch, most of the volunteers were not wealthy, so they needed financial resources to launch their ministry work.

Who are the people providing financial help to launch social and religious sector causes these days? The answer is the parachurch. That is, the organizations that provide microfinances for mission and ministry are primarily the effort of ordinary people who launched an organization for the purpose of providing a service to people who want to build a business for ministry's sake. Funding might come from churches that desire to help, but it also comes from private individuals. In other words, microfinance is not the result of any one established church, but rather the result of the grassroots church.

One such organization is Opportunity International. They provide microfinance loans, savings, and insurance as well as training in financial management. And in tune with the times, at their core is holistic development: the economic, social, and spiritual transformation of the poor, their families, and their communities. They exist to develop local leadership capacity and strengthen the social and spiritual fabric of communities through economic development.

THE INTERMEDIARY ORGANIZATION

Now that donor giving is increasingly going directly to overseas ministries, it is challenging for donors to build good relationships with funding recipients to know if their money is used effectively. In the past they relied on a church or mission agency to provide due diligence. Now they are bypassing the agencies and giving directly. This means they have an increased responsibility to ensure that they are giving wisely and effectively, but this often requires expertise and personal relationships with the foreign funding recipients.

Conversely, ministries desiring to make a funding appeal need to demonstrate to the direct givers that they have a clear vision, well-thought-out plans, and self-monitoring methods worked out. Who can assist them with project design and accountability planning to produce compelling proposals to donors? In other words, it takes a lot of time and expertise to prepare good proposals. It also takes people who can evaluate those proposals to ensure good planning on the one hand and good use of money on the other. These are some reasons why expert intermediary help between the donor and their potential funding recipient will become more common, and that need has birthed the intermediary organization.

In the for-profit sector, a middleman provides business to business services, such as consulting, advising, and analyzing. These are typical areas where a business lacks expertise. The goal of middlemen is to help their client be successful and, of course, produce a healthy profit from their own business venture. Now this sort of expert intermediary help is creating value for donors and recipients in the non-profit sector. The intermediary fulfills the expert gaps that donors and the recipients have. Through their service, intermediary organizations help build a stronger relationship between donors and funding recipients to achieve success in their philanthropic and ministerial goals.

One thing that distinguishes the new parachurch intermediary organizations from their business world counterpart, is that they are doing this as ministry and not for financial profit or fame. This is what social sector authors Matthew Bishop and Michael Green refer to as the "virtuous middlemen," experts working through alliance partnerships purely for the good of others. That is, "They can help funders figure out their values, agree on strategies, evaluate options, do their due diligence, and monitor the impact of their giving" (Bishop and Green 2008, 28). Their area of service helps donors and funding recipients build effective partnerships to achieve the greatest possible results in what they do. A caveat is that the intermediary organization doesn't assume the role of gatekeeper for the donor, unless the donor requests such a role. Because direct relations between donor and recipient are now more desirable, the intermediary organization helps such relationships come to fruition. Evidence for growth in intermediary services is the number of Gen X donors contributing through third party organizations in comparison to Baby Boomers—about 27 percent of Gen X donors and 17 percent of Baby Boomer donors (Bhagat, Loeb, and Rovner 2010).

Intermediary organizations value knowledge, and they practice knowledge management for the purpose of performance and especially innovation. Research provides knowledge, and knowledge management provides insights for both donors and funding recipients. An added value of intermediary service is helping donors and recipients understand each other's context, which, as we saw in chapter 2 ("Spending Money"), is an important thing to establish at the start of a project funding relationship.

One fast-growing intermediary organization in the area of Bible translation is the Seed Company.[22] Their parachurch role is to help financial givers and ministry workers labor together in satisfying and effective ways by providing expert due diligence for donors and project

---

22 For full disclosure, the author of this book has served in a voluntary (i.e. financially self-supporting) role with The Seed Company since 2004.

design and accountability planning for ministries. An overarching goal of their service is brokering a healthy and lasting relationship between donors and funding recipients. This creates value for the people who the donor and the ministry desire to help. Once connections between the donor and their field partners are established and the project is well underway, the Seed Company prefers a reduced intermediary role so direct relationships between the donor and the field partner can flourish.

The emergence of specialist, intermediary, and training organizations is evidence that the grassroots church is yet again showing its creative and action-oriented DNA in the twenty-first century. Could this realignment have something to do with what Jesus said about working for the best possible return on what God has given the church to invest—things such as people, money, time, technology, and creativity? And make no mistake about it, these so-called parachurch organizations are a living and active part of the global church, even if they are not closely linked to any particular church denomination.

5
MISSION REINVENTION—IS IT POSSIBLE?

The Complacent

Are we to assume older parachurch ministries are simply going to fade away like the flowers of summer? Change management guru John Kotter says convincing people of the need to change is much harder when they feel no sense of urgency to do so (Kotter 1995, 60). In the for-profit world, a steep decline in financial revenues is an urgent situation. A loss in revenue is the typical outcome when business practices no longer align with the times. This gets people's attention. They are usually left with two options: create new systems and processes to improve revenue or close down the business. Kotter tells his clients that a fresh vision is a good start for realignment. It makes clear the direction in which the organization needs to go, and that helps them know what needs to change.

Social sector and faith-based non-profit organizations don't exist to generate financial revenues. They exist to generate social and spiritual outcomes, and generating income is a necessary activity. A loss in revenue is a serious problem for non-profit agencies too. The question is, how do they respond to the loss? They may change their messaging, update the look of their website, hire more fundraisers, put on more fundraising events, and increase direct mail campaigns. One thing they tend not to do is spend time talking with donors, partners, outside experts, and the people their organization serves to find out why income is down.

They may not understand that simple complacency is the root of their problems. With faith-based ministries, a family-like environment makes people comfortable. They settle into routines and practices that are familiar. Over time they begin to realize that the world is changing, but rather than figure out how to remain effective in a changing world, they figure out how to maintain the familiar comfort of their organization. As John Kotter says, unless they create a sense of real urgency, nothing is likely to change. He reassures people by saying, "Higher rate of urgency does not imply ever present panic, anxiety, or fear." Rather, it means that people are always addressing problems, responding to opportunities, and not putting things off until later (Kotter 2012, loc. 2257). In other words, work hard to figure it out.

One of Jesus' money parables is found in the Gospel of Luke, chapter 16. He tells the story of a corrupt business manager who gets fired over the questionable use of his boss' money. It seems odd that Jesus would use the example of a corrupt manager, but one part of the parable seems clear enough: even a corrupt manager was smart enough to figure out how to survive! Was Jesus telling his disciples to also be shrewd in carrying out Kingdom work?

How are mission agencies surviving these days? Do they feel any sense of urgency to change because of the times? A 2013 survey of mission CEOs found that relations with donors ranked second highest in the area of external forces most likely to impact their organization. Finances and the global economy ranked as their highest concern. Personnel retention and productivity ranked lowest (Missio Nexus 2013). With productivity as the lowest concern, how will they address their first and second highest concerns? This sounds like an urgent situation.

What Do Other Mission CEOs Think?

At a North American mission leaders conference in 2012, staff from William Carey International University hosted a breakfast for agency leaders. Part of this breakout session included an informal survey. They asked the participants, "If you could be granted three wishes for your agency in the next ten years, what would those wishes be?"

Among their responses, three areas stood out: they desire a new funding model; they need to become more internationalized; and corporate leadership structures need to change. Perhaps we should not be surprised by this forward-looking wish list. After all, the conference theme was "Reset." Participants were there to figure out how to move their agencies and church missions programs into the twenty-first century. Even so, let's examine their wish list.

A NEW FUNDING MODEL

While some agency leaders may simply wish for people to give more money to their work, the breakfast eaters understood that asking for more money through more events and increased direct mail campaigns is not likely to produce sustainable growth for their agency in the long term. They are probably right. The old tried-and-true methods of faith-based fundraising are becoming less effective as the new donors—Gen X and their children, the Millennium generation—begin giving away the trillions of dollars they now control.

A new funding model is required because the new donors' values, interests, and desires differ significantly from many, if not most, previous generation donors. They assume clear planning, benchmarks, measurable outcomes, qualitative impact, mutual accountability, innovation, acceleration, and partnership. No doubt some donors of the past held the same values, but by and large, those values are not what shaped mission agency strategies. Most donors simply trusted the experts to achieve good results. Even so, agency leaders didn't typically seek out advice and guidance from the donors. This model will not produce financial growth, thus the breakfast thinkers' wisdom—they desire a new model to align with the new realities of fundraising.

BECOME MORE INTERNATIONALIZED

Just look less American. What is wrong with a mission agency looking like America? By this, the survey respondents are simply acknowledging that Christianity is now an international faith with a diversity of expressions. In fact, the majority of Christians do not live in North America and Europe. They live in Africa, Asia, the Pacific, and Latin America. They make up over 60 percent of Christians in the world, yet they only receive 17 percent of all Christian income.

The church in these global regions has capable leadership, resources, and skills to carry out Great Commission work. They can focus on social and spiritual transformation in their own home and in other places. If a Western mission agency has official or unofficial presence in any of these countries, their future success depends greatly on their ability to serve alongside local believers in these places in useful ways.

These days, most of science and industry are moving to creative processes where open collaboration, risk taking, accelerated innovation, external learning, and technology drive their work. A traditional top-down, closed system—where creativity is reduced to what can be captured on a white board in a meeting room—is no longer the corporate model of leadership. Leaders are still needed; managers and implementers still have a job, but the leader's role now is to ensure that all of these areas are functioning so that results are happening. Hard as this may sound, many Western mission agencies of the past sixty years applied the same corporate CEO model that businesses did at the time. Are these new corporate values useful for mission agencies these days too? The breakfast meeting survey respondents seem to think so.

NEW RECRUITMENT MODELS

This relates to agencies becoming more international. The survey respondents understand that simply recruiting and sending more Americans is no longer the best use of their time, money, and areas of expertise. The best use of these resources is to multiply them in the same way that Jesus talked about in the parable of the talents.[23]

Therefore, recruiting local (i.e. national) trainers, workers, and leadership in the countries where they work is a way to achieve greater results with the resources God has entrusted to these agencies. Rather than sending more Americans to do what the local churches are already capable of doing, they desire to build an organization that is truly global and local. That requires increasing the local over the global. Better ways of partnering with global organizations are replacing the recruit-and-send model of the past.

---

23 Matthew 3:24.

Mission Agencies That Are Changing

It was mentioned that the respondents to this informal survey were participants at a "Reset" conference, thus it is safe to assume they already have a bias for innovative change. Are other agency leaders wishing for the same things? Are they doing more wishing than actually instituting change? Consider the following results of another survey (Gravelle 2013).

Leaders of three mission organizations that had or were in the process of instituting significant changes were asked why they were doing that. This survey sampling was more specified. It applied more poignant questions, which led to additional questions. One organization was an old mainline denomination, another a more modern parachurch agency, and the third an established businessmen's parachurch agency.

The following five questions were used to generate deeper discussions on these topics, thus this was not a random, controlled sampling, but rather an open, dialogue-oriented interview.

1. Why is your agency initiating change now?
2. What areas are you changing?
3. How important are historical agency values and legacy amidst change?
4. How are finances (use of money) affected by this change?
5. How is staff affected by the way your agency is changing?

ON INSTITUTING CHANGE

Mutuality was one key reason why these agency leaders desire organizational change. As one leader expressed it, "The church (overseas) is able to carry out work that we have traditionally done." They talked about partnership. "We've noted the rise in capable like-minded ministries who carry out discipleship and evangelism, but who don't have the materials needed to support those activities. That's where we help." Another leader used the phrase "beneficial mutual learning" and talked about how Western mission agencies used to prescribe but never viewed themselves as learners. One agency leader told how he brought in researchers to help his group understand how much significant change their organization needed. The group thought, perhaps, that he was only exaggerating things.

The Bible League International (BLI), for example, is moving towards a service model, providing Scripture material to local churches and ministries to carry out church planting activities rather than doing church planting themselves. What is the difference? Under the new strategy, they are supporting locally run programs rather than their own. As a result, local organizations increase in capacity to carry out the Great Commission in their own region and beyond.

After 125 years of mission history, Christian Reformed World Missions (CRWM) decided it was time for change. Joel Hogan, Director of International Ministries for CRWM, relates that in 2007, CRWM leadership had an epiphany. Realizing how the center of Christianity was no longer located in the West, they believed it was time for CRWM to humbly partner with the strong and vital churches and institutions that God was raising up all around the world. CRWM decided to change their focus from a sending agency to primarily a partnership focused agency.

However, they decided that they would not partner with agencies that depended on them for survival. Instead, they wanted to partner with churches and Christian organizations that were already strong and doing effective ministry. These organizations were capable of further strengthening their own capacity, but the partnership provided ways to do even more together. As Hogan put it, "As much as possible, we want to take control and power issues off the table."

Mission agency leaders may be hesitant to move their mission in dramatically new directions because of a perceived threat to their agency's legacy. In most cases, their legacy is one to be proud of. People have supported mission agencies just because of their good reputation built on a lasting legacy over the years. Usually, a new leader was chosen precisely because he or she would continue building on their agency's legacy. Legacy is a good thing if the practices they build on are well-aligned with the times, but what if they are not? We asked these innovating mission leaders about the importance of legacy.

For 125 years, Christian Reformed World Missions worked to establish Christian Reformed churches (CRC) around the world. Because of their denomination's legacy, they did not often interact with church denominations other than Reformed or Presbyterian churches. Now they are no longer interested in planting new CRC churches. Instead, they partner with many denominations. "We continue to value a confessionally Reformed understanding, but we don't need to partner with only Reformed churches. In fact, 30 percent of our partners are not Reformed churches," says Joel Hogan.

They haven't given up their Reformed legacy, but they are giving up independence and exclusivity in their missions work. Hogan further states, "The major wisdom was that the world has changed, and we realized that we also needed to change in order to be relevant as a global mission agency." It's remarkable for an organization with a 125-year-old legacy in denominational missions.

For Bible League International (BLI), their core purpose remains the same. "It is still about helping people have access to Scripture in a language and reading level that they can use and understand." Like most Western agencies, their legacy practice was for Bible League workers to do it all. Now that service is coming through partners and other ministries. As BLI's Carol Dowsett put it, "What matters is seeing the word of God planted in people's lives by those best positioned to do that. Increasingly that is the local church and ministries." One could say that their new partners are building on their age-old legacy goals for even greater Scripture impact.

INCREMENTAL OR SWEEPING CHANGES?

Other mission agencies are facing pressure these days. Typically, the pressure comes from at least two groups: donors and younger generation workers. Historically, it is the donors who first recognize when a mission agency or sending church is losing its effectiveness. And because the agency and church leaders do not usually take their concerns into consideration, the donors move their money to where it will have greater effect. In response to income loss, some agencies apply incremental changes to show they are keeping up with the times. Yet incremental change doesn't display the sort of progressive thinking donors are looking for. The times require more rapid adjustments.

Each new generation of Western mission workers operates with a different set of values. The emerging generation workers may not, by and large, hold to the same rugged individualist and independent-minded moral beliefs of the previous generation. They want to work in teams. They are not motivated by long, open-ended efforts with no completion in sight. Rather, they prefer to focus on tangible causes that are measurable. And because they were shaped by the age of innovation, witnessing creative surges in technology and entertainment, they assume the same should be applied to mission endeavors. Therefore, they are more likely to start their own grassroots mission effort than join an agency that does not share their values. How do agency leaders respond to the sort of disruptive entrepreneurship younger workers are bringing to missions these days? It seems there are two rather stark choices. They can tap into this new creative energy or they can alienate it.

Speaking of disruptive entrepreneurship, take the young leaders of The Gideons International In Canada. The Gideons organization was founded in 1899. In the United States, they claim to be the oldest association of Christian businessmen and professionals. That also makes them a long-lasting parachurch organization. They are best known for placing Bibles in hotel rooms. At the start, the idea seemed natural because the first members of the Gideons were traveling businessmen who spent a lot of time in hotels. They saw the hotels as their mission field. When it comes to legacy practices, The Gideons are staying close to founding principles. However, things are going in new directions with The Gideons affiliate in Canada.

As Giorgio Gori, director of development for The Gideons International In Canada, puts it, changing their mission and methods is like rebuilding a Boeing aircraft while flying. Legacy practices continue, but rebuilding to be more effective these days is happening fast. Even so, these changes come at a cost, such as becoming a separate organization to institute the changes they desire. Another cost is not being able to use the name Gideons International in their foreign work. What are the changes that more or less isolate them from the international organization?

The changes are sweeping, and they believe the changes are necessary in the West, which they consider to be post-Christian. A post-

Christian West doesn't engage with Scripture the traditional Gideons way by finding a printed Bible left by The Gideons in hotel rooms. Now The Gideons in Canada is focusing on multiple distribution schemes, and social media is central.

Understanding that language changes, too, they have shifted from only giving the New American Standard Bible version to giving the New Living Translation. Additionally, a different vision of ministry with their brothers to the south led to The Gideons in Canada welcoming Christians of all vocations as full participants. In The Gideons International, women are still considered supporting members.

In the traditional model, the printed Bible was the evangelist. The assumption was that people would find the Bible in a hotel room, read it, encounter God, and then become new believers. There is no doubt that is exactly what happened many times. But because impact evaluation did not focus on follow-up and discipleship per se, no one really knew how many of those people found a church, became disciples, and grew in knowledge of the Bible they freely received.

Success was measured by the number of Bibles given out. And with this model, more Bibles had to be given out each year to ensure growth and success. But as Gori asked, how many of those Bibles ended up in a trash can shortly after? He recalled how he saw a number of Bibles given to students at a school event end up in the trash can shortly after the event ended, yet Gideons workers still had to report the number of Bibles given out.

The Gideons International In Canada wants to move from Bible distribution to Bible impact. That requires a shift in operating strategies. They still want to give Bibles, but more directly, with more personal involvement and follow-up. Measuring success will have more to do with how many of the people receiving Bibles find a church home and build relations with other believers. If there is no movement on this cline, success has not been achieved yet.

These Gideons also understand the importance of collective impact. That means they work with other agencies with feet on the ground in places like Haiti, for example. This strengthens both organizations' chances of achieving greater results together than they could individually.

Usually, organization affiliates are afraid to buck tradition and reinvent themselves for relevancy in a way that prevents them from using the organization's name. This is because name recognition usually brings trust, and that brings traditional funding opportunities. Not so with The Gideons International In Canada. They risked losing name affiliation because of their vision for discipleship and impact. Their vision is the world, but they are not allowed to use the name The Gideons outside of Canada. New branding and naming is necessary, but they aren't afraid to go this route. Indeed, they are shifting to a lean operating model, one that makes use of outside expertise rather than developing all areas of expertise within their organization. This gives them more freedom and flexibility to adapt to a changing world. They are developing an economy of scope rather than scale.

They are not as interested in expanding their footprint in other countries as much as they are in building capacity in other people to do the same work. They want to invest in partner organizations, especially the local church in other countries, passing on training, experience, and ability to those entities. Doing this makes achieving greater impact more possible. Therefore, they have a strong focus on forming strategic partnerships with several organizations instead of going it alone.

The Gideons International In Canada is one organization demonstrating that it is indeed possible to reinvent an old, venerable parachurch organization—or are they? Instead, maybe they are forced to invent a totally new organization because the parent organization was not willing to make the changes needed to achieve impact in ways The Gideons International In Canada envision. The new Gideons International In Canada demonstrate a closer relationship between business people and church ministers, as if there is no ministry and laity division at all. Rather it is the church on mission, working together to achieve spiritual change as people engage with God through his word, using multimedia in dynamic and relevant ways.

HOW IS MONEY A FACTOR?

The last survey question asked was, "When it comes to missions and money, what are your agencies' values and best practices?" In other words, how were these mission agencies using finances in the new scheme of things? As far as our limited conversation revealed, no organization seemed to view the use of money as a highly significant part of their reinvention strategy.

One leader did have this to say: "We did too many things to hurt people with money when we tried to help. We came with too much resources too fast. Now we've changed to asking them through a conversation to take a blessings inventory. Decide together how they can maximize those blessings—their assets, food, material goods, labor, plant crops—with a section dedicated to the church." It's a good start. Begin with what God has already amply provided among the people and assist them in areas that supplement what they have to contribute.

Perhaps the lack of concrete responses to the strategic use of money relates to the assumption people have that donors will just continue trusting the agencies with the wise and effective use of the money they provide. Western mission strategists have not generally viewed the role of money as a part of missiology. Mostly, they have complained about how money has driven mission, as it has at times. Still, it is a mistake for any agency working on reinvention to not think through how the allocation of funds will help to achieve outcome and impact goals.

In regard to strategies, one could pose questions such as, how much of your funds is used to maintain your organization, including your field staff? How are the funds creating more income, especially among the people you serve? How much is going towards experimentation and innovation? Money shouldn't be the sole driver of strategies, but money is a resource given by God to achieve his purposes, and that to the greatest extent possible.

This small survey sampling was done with organizations that are taking action to align organizational practices with twenty-first century realities. While the changes these organizations are instituting can be applauded, work remains to be done. The ratio of Western to non-Western missionaries in Christian lands needs to be seriously addressed. Western agency leadership needs to more seriously and rigorously reconsider the financial and human cost outlay in terms of overall mission effectiveness. Partnership alliances are important, but that means Western agencies willingly give up some of their strongly held practices so that the alliance can be strengthened.

If a mission agency's goal is to make disciples, among other biblical mandates, then leadership needs to assess how their current methods are achieving this measureable outcome from time to time. Because of globalization, technological advances, and donor attitude shift, re-evaluation needs to occur more frequently at some level, and that possibly every three to five years.

The Demise of Long-term Mission

While some mission agencies take on the hard work of reinvention for relevancy, another trend may actually point to their eventual demise. Western mission is in a great state of flux these days. This century is known as the globalized period in mission. After two thousand years of Great Commission missionary work, culminating with two hundred years of modern Western mission expansion, traditional missionary receiving countries now have significantly large Christian populations. The majority of Christians now live in Africa, Asia, Latin America, and the Pacific, and their church expressions are as diverse as the number of unique cultural and linguistic groups there are in those places.

Figure 2. Number of Christians by Region (Millions)

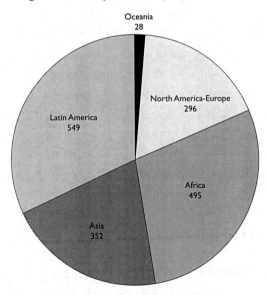

This demographic and global shift brings mission shift. This means that while the overarching goals of planting churches and making disciples may be the same, the preferred practices, methods, and even outcomes Global South (i.e. non-Western) Christians desire are increasingly divergent from Western assumptions.

Figure 3. Global South Church Goals

Personal dimension perspective
Tangible remedies, social reactions
Transformation
Creative presentations (non-confrontational)
Scripture acted out through multiple media methods
Group response within cultural context
Urgent pastoral views
Development from a holistic perspective, all interrelated (physical, social justice)
Locally relevant training
Hermeneutical communities—local theologies

Figure 3 illustrates some of these divergent areas. Mission shift requires Western mission agencies and donors to consider how this disjunction in mission impact goals relates to the use of mission agency funds and philanthropy. Are the billions of dollars currently spent on Western mission work a wise use of the funds?

Moreover, the majority of Western long-term missionaries are working in traditional missionary receiving lands. This means that about 85 percent of Christian evangelism is aimed at Christians in these places, while there is almost no interaction with followers of other major world religions in the non-Christian countries. And it cost $163 billion annually to maintain these workers in the Christian lands (Johnson and Ross 2009).

Figure 4 reveals that about $13 billion is spent annually on sending long-term missionaries overseas. Although the figure works out to be about $42,000 annually per family unit, the cost would be higher if agency administrative cost and ministry maintenance and fundraising were included. The cost per family unit may be surprising when compared to what a national church organization ministry could do with the same amount of money. The dollar impact is lessened with the traditional sending model. Moreover, the $13 billion figure is a disproportionally large amount of Western mission funds spent on the sending and maintaining of foreign mission presence in lands that have proportionally more Christians than the sending countries have.

Figure 4. Annual Cost of Foreign Mission Sending as of 2010

Foreign sending to Christian lands	306,000 (73.1% of workforce)	$13 billion
Foreign sending to unreached lands	10,200	$250 million

These long-term Western workers are going to serve Christians that are said to adhere more closely to handed-down apostolic teaching than the Western Christian countries do. In comparison, the unreached countries receive significantly fewer missionaries, resulting in a lower use of mission funds. This is not surprising given the closed or limited access to these countries. Even less is spent on equipping and supporting the minority church presence in those unreached places.

HIGH COST WITH LOW RETURNS

The Christian population of traditional missionary sending countries (in North America and Western Europe) now stands at an estimated 296 million. In 1910, these countries contained 80 percent of the world's Christians. Now they contain only 20 percent. Yet the number of long-term missionaries sent by foreign agencies from these countries to traditional receiving countries has increased by 5.64 percent over the last ten years. However, factoring in people leaving long-term missions means the growth rate is generally flat.[24] In many cases, the new long-term missionaries are

---

24 Personal involvement is a growing trend among Gen X and Mosaics. Short-term missions is surging at the rate of about 26 percent growth a year in the US, while long-term mission growth remains rather flat. Missionaries are also leaving the field to care for aging parents, but they maintain participation from home (Moreau 2008, 1–33).

applying traditional Western practices that no longer align well with the Global South church values given early in Figure 3. Does this indicate that a neocolonial understanding of missions ("the West to the rest") is still implicitly understood by the long-term mission agencies?

Western mission agencies see this global Christianity shift occurring, and they say that it's time for the church in these lands to take over leadership in evangelism, church planting, and Bible translation. However, as mission professor Lois Douglas asks, "What have we left them to lead with?" (Douglas 2006, 277). Douglas asks this question because the resources and methods brought by Western mission agencies to foreign lands are fast losing practical usefulness and relevancy during this indigenous church growth period in church history. This means that most of the Western mission funds spent on sending workers to the mission field annually are not creating sufficient beneficial growth and impact in the places the missionaries serve.

How could Western donors and the workers they support see greater results in the funds they spend and the hours of work they put in?

1. Invest in national and Western mission agencies that focus primarily on training national church partners. The outcome is accelerated capacity building so that those Christians can launch, nurture, and sustain missionary movements within their own lands and the lands of their close neighbors, especially the unreached groups.

2. Change the spending ratio. The majority of Western mission funds should directly benefit the majority world churches' ability to carry out their work with access to more relevant resource materials, training methods, project management, and expansion work. These are some areas for which funding would produce greater beneficial impact.

3. Significantly increase national church missions funding. More funds should empower national church efforts in unreached regions and countries.

4. Reduce the sending of Western missionaries. Long-term sending to traditional receiving Christian lands

to do things in the same ways they were done in the past needs to be dramatically reduced. This will free up billions of dollars that can be redirected to capacity building of Christian ministries in those lands.

Short-term Missions: The Reinvention of Western Mission?

The rise of world Christianity and the decline in long-term missions sending from the West provides a backdrop for considering the emerging and difficult-to-explain phenomenon of short-term missions.

The short-term missions (STM) movement does not appear to be a short-lived trend. Research indicates that between 1996 and 2005 the average annual growth rate of people participating in STM was about 27 percent. This rate of growth caused STM to increase by about 218 percent during this period (Moreau 2008). According to a 2006 study, up to 1.6 million people per year from North America were going on short-term missions trips (Priest 2006). The average length of a trip by that time was about ten to fourteen days long. What was the cost of these trips spent in the name of missions?

This topic should not be viewed simply in terms of a cost-benefit analysis, although that is a legitimate concern. For example, an STM group went to Haiti at the cost of $1,500 per person to build a house for poor Haitians in a region that had 80 percent unemployment. Another STM group spent $30,000 in combined travel cost to build one $2,000 house there. Yet another STM group spent $29,000 to repair a church roof and build a small clinic in Guatemala. They returned home with stories about how much they enjoyed their trip (Stravers 2012, 43).

The point is that individuals and organizations who give financially to mission endeavors do so with the expectation that good and lasting results will occur, in part, because of their financial involvement. They are accountable to God and people for the good use of those funds. STM workers are also accountable for the effect their funds have on a mission project. Mission agencies, churches, and individuals are also accountable for the strategic use of funds, and for using them in ways that align well with the times. The figure below shows the rate of local and foreign STM and the associated cost of those missions trips.[25]

Figure 5. Cost of Short-term Home and Foreign Missions

	People involved in STM	Avg. Cost Per Person	Annual Cost
Home	30% (48,000 people)	$650	$31.2 million
Foreign	70% (1.552 million people)	$2,000	$3.1 billion
		Total Cost	**$3.44 billion**

IS STM CHURCH MISSION?

A number of professional mission strategists, known as missiologists, and long term missionaries question whether STM is indeed "missions." However, the critics' biggest concern is that STM workers rush off to foreign lands with little to no cross-cultural training or effective planning to do good for others. Missiologist Robert Priest summarized the prevailing view among these critics by saying, "STM is a populist movement with minimal connection either to missiology or to seminary education" (Priest 2006).

Although STM is still a relatively new movement, it should not be discredited just because it is a grassroots movement. Status quo leaders (mostly clergy) at the time of William Carey (1761–1834), and later the massive student volunteer movement of the nineteenth century, dismissed these grassroots efforts as unofficial and unprofessional. They labeled them "parachurch." These movements eventually launched the expansive twentieth-century Western missions era. Now the Gen X and Mosaic generations are generally bypassing traditional sending agencies. Clearly change is happening again, and early change is typically messy and somewhat chaotic. Additionally, it is premature to question STM practices in light of current mainstream missions "best practices," because some of these practices are no longer the best for these times either.

---

25 See Priest 2006. Priest provided the percentage. The author of this volume provided the average cost.

WHAT DO STM WORKERS DO?

The authors of one book define STM as "non-professional guest workers" carrying out activities in four categories: evangelism, witnessing, discipleship, and helps (Priest 2008). The book contributors describe numerous activities they say fall under these four areas. In other words, the sorts of activities found in STM literature (see figure 6 below) could fall into any one of the four categories deemed "missions." What effects do these areas of activity have on mission?

One website promotes "adventures" in missions. The trips are custom-designed for youth groups, high school groups, adults, college students, and families. They even offer an around-the-world adventure doing missions. At this level, STM is marketed as a consumer product. Other consumer-oriented STM websites abound. Some critics suggest this consumer notion is also what drives STM with churches. STM volunteers are involved in an amazing variety of activities reckoned by them as missions. These areas include the following short list of activities found in STM literature.

Figure 6. Areas of Short-term Mission Service

Construction	Medical	Literacy
Maintenance	Food relief	Mission training
Financial	Disaster relief	Discipleship
Clerical	Children's ministry	Church planting
Technological	Orphanage support	Music
Recording	Film	Drama

CLAIMS OF BENEFICIAL IMPACT

People involved in STM claim that a lot of good comes out of their trips. However, there are few quality research reports that validate these claims. One researcher reported that there were only thirteen quality studies out of forty studies examined. All thirteen studies showed no noticeable beneficial change claimed in two significant missions categories: increased giving and long-term going.

Figure 7. Benefit of Short-term Missions

Benefit for STM Workers	Benefit for Advancing Missions	Benefit for People Served
Increased cross-cultural understanding	Increased missions giving	?
Improved global church relations	Increased long-term mission going	?
Personal spiritual development	Greater prayer for missions	?
More willing to work cross-culturally at home	Improved global church relations	?
Increased ability to educate home church members	?	?

Evaluation of the benefits to STM workers listed in column 1 showed no clear evidence that these changes had occurred, even in small numbers. Reports for column 3 were generally anecdotal (Peterson 2003).

The third column in the figure above is empty. It's not because STM workers can't claim beneficial results for the people they served. It seems to be because they don't really know what sorts of lasting effects their STM work contributed. They only know what happened during the short time they were there. Columns 1 and 2 tend to be areas of more tangible justifications intended for critics of STM. These sorts of results are mentioned more often in surveys and articles (Ver Beck 2008, 480).

Based on this survey sampling, it appears for now that results given in columns 1 and 2 are not significant factors. If all three categories of beneficial impact claimed by STM cannot be confirmed quantitatively and qualitatively, then what is the benefit of the $3.44 billion spent on STM?

Some people claim that most STM funding comes from family, friends, and churches who might not otherwise give to missions. Even so, considering that the funds are given in the name of missions, usually as a tax-deductible gift, the givers are still accountable. They are accountable for good results to church missions, to the people the STM effort serves, and even to the US or Canadian government, because charitable tax deductions come with stated expectations.

STM IS DIRECT INVOLVEMENT

The previous period of evangelical mission focused primarily on proclamation and transmission of Scripture knowledge, with less emphasis on addressing physical and social needs. The most significant shift in mission now is STM doing less of these traditional mission activities and more relief and development work.

Mission strategy professionals believe STM is more about personal spiritual growth and discipleship learning for the volunteer, and perhaps less so for Great Commission mission. Even so, the rapid growth in STM is a significant indicator of the times. People are increasingly uninterested in traditional Western long-term mission. Therefore, not only are people beginning to give directly and globally, but they are also going directly and globally to participate in the work, even if it is only for fourteen days. For the givers and goers, it provides immediate impact.

The link that appears to be missing in all of this is the global to local link. An important result of STM these days is for the travelers to bring back a better understanding of mission "over there," specifically how the majority world church is on mission. This suggests that STM, during this interval in Western mission history, could be more of a fact-finding effort. This is needed because, as discussed in the previous section, official church and parachurch mission in the West is generally out of touch with what is happening in the majority world of Africa, Asia, the Pacific, and Latin America.

So while the Western church is figuring out what an updated role in global mission would be, short-term missions could also help if more people participated in global mission from home, where their activities can have effects overseas. This may not sound glamorous to young volunteers compared to a trip to Uganda. However, if beneficial change is the goal, then STM workers can produce greater and longer lasting effects serving in the following seven areas.

SEVEN WAYS FOR STM TO BE MORE EFFECTIVE

Reach the Unreached at Home

Recent migrants from the last-reached people groups are living in your neighborhoods. The results of STM efforts here at home will spread to their extended families still living in these unreached places in Africa, Asia, and the Middle East. See the book *Strangers Next Door* (Payne 2012).

Equip Students and Guest Workers

Students and professionals studying and working in the US can be equipped to return to their home countries to carry out effective home missions there. Resources can be found at www.intervarsity.org.

Advocate for People on the Margins

Generate long-term support through social advocacy and social media. It is amazing to consider that, with internet access so easy, with cell phones so ubiquitous, the voices of those suffering injustice and persecution around the world are not often represented by media outlets in the US. The Web provides abundant information. It just takes someone to bring that information to the attention of more people in the US and Canada.

Develop Partnership Alliances

Independence is not a virtue in the global era of mission. Greater impact can happen when STM agencies collaborate with other like-minded agencies.

Be Global Missions Smart

If you want to participate in foreign missions overseas, be more intentional about serving a church or mission organization in the countries where STM visits occur. Assist them in achieving their goals. Help them develop greater capacity in needed areas of expertise. Develop more long-term relationships to generate more lasting results.

Learn Effective Development Principles

If you want your time and money to count, then learn how to help without hurting. How would you apply what you bring in a way that enables the people you serve to lift themselves from impoverishments that plague them? See the book *When Helping Hurts* (Corbett and Fikkert 2009).

Make International Justice Needs More Widely Known

People don't suffer injustice outside of the United States only. It's a global problem for the global church. What you do to help here could also help the world. The International Justice Mission is one organization that focuses on this area.

Now the pendulum is swinging toward STM, perhaps too far. For those involved in relief work, measuring beneficial impact will be required to justify short-term missions cost. It also means holistic strategies will need to be examined in terms of how they actually help local people improve their lives.

6
FROM OUTCOMES TO IMPACT: THE NEW DONOR FOCUS

Over the last several years, social sector and faith-based organizations advertised themselves as outcome-oriented. Many agencies used something called a logic model to deliver results. Planning for desired outcomes followed a logical flow. The process addressed things such as inputs and producing outputs, which were needed to create the desired outcomes. The outcomes are things that constitute success. For example, addressing the concern of children having no parents at home when they return from school led to the idea of establishing after-school programs in ten schools. Activities, e.g., the inputs, such as money raised and staff hired, led to the outputs, such as a coherent plan with steps for implementation. This led to the final outcome: ten after-school programs were established, and now the students had a safe place to wait until their parents came home.

An example of this sort of planning in the faith-based sector would be generally the same. A church-planting organization raises funds and enlists people who are discipled and trained to plant churches. When training and equipping is complete, the trainees are sent to start new churches. New churches are the outcome. For Bible translation agencies, a successful outcome has typically been a completed New Testament translation.

Successful completion of these sorts of projects is the outcome. It is something tangible and thus quantifiable. Therefore, it seemed natural that counting the outcomes was the way the agencies reported success. This understanding led to quantification metrics. The assumption was, the larger amount of the outcome, the greater the success of the endeavor. With Christian ministry, counting new churches, new believers, people baptized, number of film showings, responses recorded, tracts distributed, and Bible translations completed was about as far as agencies went in demonstrating success. Project donors were generally content with this sort of program validation.

Some Christian ministries applied a little more rigor in program evaluation by adopting scientific metrics from the social sector. They conducted surveys using a Likert scale to understand degrees of success. They utilized multiple choice questionnaires, arranged focus group discussions, and conducted one-on-one interviews, using a standardized question form. Standardization was important to scientifically validate the findings.

What Difference Did It Make?

People have not typically sought to measure changes in a person's life because of a project. This is qualitative change. What difference did an after-school program make in the lives of the students, their parents, or their home life? For Christian ministries, how did the presence of a new church affect individual lives and community life? When a New Testament was translated, how did having access to printed Scripture change people and eventually situations? Of course, most people carry out these sorts of projects because they do want to improve people's lives. A significant bet is that the program will indeed have the intended result.

Outward indicators that something positive happened in a person's life are not difficult to find, but they are only observations at best, which generates lots of assumptions at worst. Assumptions have to be tested, therefore getting into someone's heart and mind is necessary to discover what the social sector calls "phenomenon change" and the faith sector calls "spiritual change."

These days, donors are increasingly interested in knowing about this sort of change, but spiritual or phenomenon change seems difficult if not impossible to measure. Some people would argue that spiritual change is something God does. Therefore it is presumptuous, if not blatantly sinful, to even attempt to measure spiritual change. But this raises the question, how do agencies know their work is producing the sort of spiritual results that God expects them to produce with the resources he has provided if they are not finding ways to discover what has changed? How does a foundation know that the time, money, and effort put into a social program are producing social capital—improved societal well-being? They need to figure this out, because outward indicators of success are not as satisfying as they once were for donors and some practitioners. They need to work on discovering what is changing on the inside.

STARTING WITH THE END IN MIND

An increasingly popular way to plan projects these days is to first talk about impact. That is the ultimate change in a person's life that project planners desire to see as a result of their work. Note the focus on the word "change." It does not start with the ultimate "outcome" a planner desires to achieve. If change is the most important reason for a project, then what change is should be the first topic discussed. Some people refer to this as "impact-oriented planning."

For example, consider a Christian organization that provides free wheelchairs to disabled people in impoverished regions of the world. Giving a wheelchair to a needy disabled person is certainly an essential activity, because it leads to an immediate outcome: improved mobility. Does this sort of organization exist purely for the sake of improved mobility? Not usually. The "what difference does it make" question would be, how does improved mobility improve the person's life? Assumptions about how a wheelchair can improve a person's life are many. Increased independence raises self-esteem. Mobility expands their living environment. It could open the way for employment. Any one of these things produces positive change. But are these areas of change a natural result of giving someone a wheelchair? Many people assume they are.

A Christian ministry like this does not usually exist simply to provide a wheelchair, as nice as that is. They certainly have compassion for people who cannot afford one, but ultimately they desire something far greater than improved mobility. They desire spiritual change to happen in the person. The wheelchair is an input, an important step towards greater results.

If that is true, then an impact planning approach would start with the ultimate goal in mind. What would it take to see hundreds of needy disabled people living a more fulfilling life with spiritual hope and anticipation of good things to come? Working backwards from that question leads to probably the first step in the whole plan: providing a free wheelchair. Yet that is what people often assume is the final step. But it is just an input, a thing provided. It does not guarantee any of the things the organization desires.

A reverse logic model would first begin to address other key activities and outputs to achieve the ultimate goal. This might include relationship building, ways to connect the wheelchair recipient to work and life opportunities, providing job training, joining mutual support communities, providing spiritual guidance through prayer, counseling, and Bible study, and building a local church support network. These are seemingly all things that would provide a greater chance for success if spiritual, emotional, and physical improvements are the ultimate goals of the free wheelchair ministry.

Figure 8. Example of the Reverse Logic Model

Impact	Outcomes	Outputs	Inputs
Your ultimate goal	Necessary things produced for impact	The result of activities to produce outcomes	Things and activities to produce outputs
Examples			
(1) Physically healthy children	Eating nutritious food and exercising	Affordable nutritious food and access to playgrounds	Find ways to provide affordable healthy food and places to play
(2) Spiritual growth	Accessing and utilizing educational materials	Appropriate discipleship training resources and access	Research, learn, and develop appropriate materials and delivery methods

Program evaluation would focus on how the person has changed because of all of those things. It would not just count the number of wheelchairs distributed as an indicator of success. The story would tell the difference the total program made in the lives of the people they helped.

Figure 8 provides a simplified overview of starting with impact and working backwards to determine what is most needed to achieve success at each important phase. Going deeper into the plan would produce other layers of inputs, outputs, and outcomes, generating additional inputs, outputs, and outcomes until ultimately achieving impact. Starting with impact shapes everything to the right in the figure.

Inspecting What You Expect

These days, many organizations in the social and religious sector understand the importance of impact measurement. Counting still has value, but measurement is not necessarily just about counting things. Rather, it has more to do with observing and learning through dialogue, among other methods, and about the sorts of deep change happening as a result of the ministry project. What methods will you use to discover the areas of impact stemming from your project? It is not difficult for social and ministry workers to learn how to discover transformational change.

Figure 9. Example of Areas of Impact

Area	What to look for	How to record it
Individuals	Who is impacted by the project so far: individuals, pastors, teachers, evangelists, church planters, social workers?	Make a list of who your target audience is, and evaluate how each of those people is affected by the project.
Character change	Are there changes in people's habits, values, attitudes, practices, mutual trust, and honesty?	Write down your observations in each area where there is evidence.
Knowledge of the project	Are they behaving in the ways the project hoped to influence?	Make notes of how they are demonstrating that.
External influence	Are there more people showing interest in the areas the project is meant to serve?	Indicate through numbers and make notes of what types of people are becoming involved.
Care About Others	Are people helping others who are suffering from poverty, disease, addictions, injustice, etc.?	Make notes of who is doing that and how they are doing it.

Discussion question: By this point, the partners should know what the spiritual and physical needs of the people and their culture are, and they have designed their project to specifically address those needs. Now it is important for the partners to plan for ways to measure both physical and spiritual results. What things would be most important to measure, and how would you go about measuring those things? Figure 9 on the previous page provides some ideas to stimulate thinking. Make a chart of the areas that your project should be evaluating for spiritual and physical results.

Measuring Spiritual Change: Can It Be Done?

Spiritual or phenomenon change takes time. It may take a long time. How can someone measure spiritual or phenomenon change, or at least identify early indicators that deeper things are happening on the inside? Brenda Zimmerman, a York University professor and expert on complexity theory, once said at a conference, "It's not good enough to have scientific proof. We also need social proof." A representative of the Hewlett foundation speaking at the same conference said, "Remember the days when good intentions and anecdotes were good enough for program evaluation?"

It appears that just telling a story or presenting impressive numbers alone is losing its credibility, even among experts. In regard to reporting numbers, it is becoming downright suspect with many donors these days. Unsubstantiated wildly large numbers have created this distrust. Make no mistake, numbers can be helpful indicators of success, but these days they need to be backed up with qualitative insights.

Global mission and ministry are undergoing significant change these days, especially in the area of training, translation, theology, and hermeneutics. Many of our Western assumptions of what constitutes spiritual impact are undergoing new scrutiny. Seeking and reporting qualitative change may require very untypical methods that are not scientifically empirical. It could simply be collecting data in the form of testimonies, stories, and admissions, but a large enough sampling to see patterns.

Over the last decade, survey experts have questioned the reliability of standardized interview and focus group methods because the methods "violate the usual norms of conversational behavior. It might endanger the validity of data collected." Instead, these survey experts recommend "allowing the interviewer to talk about the questions, to offer clarifications and elaborations, and to engage in a limited form of recipient design and common-sense inference." In other words, the interviewer should engage in natural, informal, and open dialogue with the interviewee to discover stories of change. "The central organizational feature of ordinary conversation is that who talks and about what is controlled from within the conversation by the participants themselves" (Tanur 1992).

Figure 10. Ways to Measure

Types of Measurements	Area
Counting	The number of people in various categories, such as new believers, Bible study/church attendance, baptisms, church planting, community development projects, microfinance, internet downloads, and other countable areas.
Significant Stories/ Testimonies	Individual, group, church, third person accounts, etc. Collect and compare stories to understand how the project is affecting people. Then place that information in categories to see emerging patterns.
Dialogue	Ask people to respond to a prepared set of questions. This can be done individually or through a group discussion. However, be prepared to probe further, based on their responses. Compare answers from various people to see what common areas of impact emerge.
Observations of People from the Non-Christian Community	What is said of the people involved directly in the project? What is said by those who are not? Collect this information and compare.
Other Ways?	What other ways could you use to monitor and report how the translation is affecting people?

The idea is that through natural, open but guided dialogue, the interviewees may express a number of opinions and outcomes stemming from a project meant to benefit them. This is best revealed through stories. People like to tell stories and, when prompted, will do so. It's an easier way to capture complexity. The dialogue sessions are videoed for transcription.

An analyst studies the transcriptions and makes notations on anything people said that indicates it was the result of something positive or negative they experienced because of the project. Recurring themes are noted, as are unique themes. The tabulated list of impact themes is placed in a matrix table according to at least five categories: causality, relationships, networks, time and purpose, and forms of power. This is where the most significant changes mentioned are more observable. It also reveals areas of impact that are not indicated.[26]

Figure 11. Measurement through Discovery Dialogue

Dialogue Interviewee	Indicator of Change Mentioned
woman	Improved marriage
man	Changed business practices
youth (female)	Changed behavior with friends
community leader	Changed leadership behavior
man	Helping neighbors
woman	Visiting prisoners
student (male)	Studying more often
pastor	Starting new church
mother	Caring for children differently
clean water worker	Teaching illness prevention
father	Stopped gambling
neighbor	Mended relationships
pastor	Cooperating with other churches
police officer	Stopped extortion practices

This method relies on random samplings of individuals and groups, but they are not random controlled samplings (RCS) where the same exact questions are asked of each group and the same kinds of people are in each group. Rather the samplings are based on the same themes interviewers address. However, the dialogue allows for clarifications and restatements to help ensure the interviewees understand the questions and

---

26 This model draws from a similar proven method called the Most Significant Change (MSC) Technique. See Davies and Dart 2005.

why those questions are asked. More affected people from different places and settings may mention similar if not identical themes. The method can make deep change more discoverable. Tabulating the number of people who independently comment on the same or similar things begins to show a pattern of change in people's attitudes, understanding, or perceptions. These are short-term indicators of possibly long-term change.

Figure 11 gives a highly simplified and not very scientific example of collecting insights on change in people because of a project that benefited them. It is based on an informal, dialogue-oriented interview. The simple goal is to discover stories of change, and especially those that point to trends. Indicated changes would be tabulated and evaluated for patterns that may reveal trends.

A survey conducted by The Seed Company using this dialogue survey method discovered the following:[27]

- Thirty-seven percent of the people involved in the dialogue felt that understanding what causes sin, a lack of peace, and turmoil helped them know how to deal with these sorts of things.
- Seventeen percent of the people involved in the dialogue reported how knowing the gospel stories helps them understand how to live their lives differently. They also expressed more peace in their hearts.
- Fifty percent of the people involved in the dialogue expressed impact on breaking down denominational walls, loving their neighbors rather than competing with them, making friends with neighbors, more peace in the villages, and helping their family and community.

The idea behind this method is that if people feel safe to share what they have experienced, and enough of them do this, patterns of change from within can be identified. This is the sort of social or spiritual proof Professor

---

27 This is an unpublished study, December 2013. Used with permission from The Seed Company, Arlington, TX.

Zimmerman speaks of. It is the sort of qualitative understanding that can back up the numbers that agencies like to report to their donors.

CRYOUT'S SPIRITUAL IMPACT

CryOut is a faith-based non-profit organization in Seattle. They use music, dance, arts, and workshops to empower the youth, developing them to be leaders who pursue justice for themselves and others oppressed in their communities. Their ultimate reason for existence is so that individuals experience Christ's love and undergo spiritual and social transformation. To monitor how well they are doing in achieving success at the highest level, they track ten areas of observable and measurable indicators of change.

Figure 12. CryOut's Areas of Impact Evaluation

Ability and confidence	Learning to love God and their neighbor (their community)
Improved self-control	Servant leadership
Improved self-respect	Increased understanding of God
Improved self-awareness	Ability to pursue continuing education
Genuine care for others	Employability and financial independence

They establish a life baseline understanding of each student who enters the program. That is, they try to gain a deeper understanding of where a student is in terms of what he or she hopes to become. Each quarter, they evaluate how the students are doing based on the ten evaluation points. Over the course of a few years, they are able to determine if change is indeed happening, and importantly, if the program contributed to that change. If change is not evident, this too is evaluated to understand why.

Impact tracking showed progress in how people change on the inside because of their program. The following is an example.

Baseline: When she first came to CryOut she was full of anger towards men. Her poetry expressed anger in gory and violent terms, with graphic revenge. She began attending writer's workshops and giving spoken word performances at Cultivate and in the community. Over time her anger began to subside and she began expressing herself in positive terms.

Evidence of her transformational change:

- She started writing about God (increased understanding of God).
- She started talking to God and wrestling with who he is (learning to love God, learning to understand God).
- She starting writing about purity (self-improvement, self-respect, self-awareness).
- She received an award of a purity ring (self-confidence, self-control, learning to love God).
- She voluntarily joined a high school leadership group (servant leadership, genuine care about others).
- She was nominated for high school leadership council (employability, reliability).
- Her school grades dramatically improved (ability to pursue continuing education).
- She was accepted at Washington State University (ability to pursue continuing education, employability).
- She now considers herself a Christian (loving God and understanding God).
- This sort of program evaluation helps CryOut understand how their program is slowly but surely achieving impact at the highest level. It does not guarantee perfect success, but it assures the leaders that they are not wasting their time or funds either. Importantly, it helps them know when and how to adjust, if success indicators are not evident.

DISASTER VOLUNTEERS OF GHANA

Disaster Volunteers of Ghana (DIVOG) faced a challenge. Their small organization had big ideas. They were concerned about educational opportunities for students living in isolated northern villages. They believed student success rates were directly tied to the kind of educational facilities they had in the village. The lack of clean, enclosed, and secure facilities was the biggest threat. Outdoor umbrella tree education allowed for too many distractions. People came and went as they pleased. It was too easy for parents to walk up and pull their children out of class whenever they wanted their help. In addition, the government would only provide electricity to a school "building." Teacher retention rates were low in villages that did not have a school building.

DIVOG leaders believed that a certain kind of school building was essential for more students to succeed. And education was central to fulfilling their ultimate goal of seeing people lifted out of poverty. Their challenge was raising more funds to help more villagers build school buildings, because it would take far more improvements in the number of schools in this poor region to achieve their dream of poverty alleviation on a wider scale. But it would be difficult to convince more people to invest on a larger scale by only counting the number of completed school buildings. Evidence to prove their operating assumption was necessary. They needed a project impact measurement plan. It would at least show indicators of how the presence of a school building was beginning to move people along the path to better living. With help, they devised a plan.

DIVOG will conduct a survey to measure the results of their work over the last eight years for the following reasons:

1. It helps them know how the work is going, the results, and how they might improve.

2. They will know the level of poverty alleviation achieved thus far, the ultimate goal of the project.

3. They will discover the level of interest in the community and their response to opportunities.

4. By surveying the people affected, the people also see how the project affects them, and how they may need to make adjustments.

5. The information will help current and potential donors to know that their giving is having beneficial impact on people.

Quantitative Measurements Goals
- Increase in student population (before building and after building).
- Number of students who went to higher grades (before program and after program).

- Number of villages that have benefited from the school building program.
- Number of villages that built additional school buildings on their own.
- Number of schools/education institutions DIVOG has worked with.
- Number of teachers who came as a result of the school building construction.
- Number of places where electricity was provided by the government because of the school building.

Qualitative Goals
- Discover ways that village life has improved because of the school (list those ways).
- How has the student's life changed?
- How has the program affected families?
- Describe how the government has responded to villages where the school building was completed.
- How were key results from the four social domains achieved? (See previous four domains.)
- Story collection method for measuring transformation stemming from the project.

DIVOG will conduct an informal interview to ask people to tell about the project's effect on them. The idea is that they are telling you their experience through stories, hopefully, but brief answers are okay too.

Dialogue with people individually and in social networks so they feel free to answer on a personal level and as a community:
- Village leaders
- Parents
- Teachers
- Students
- Skilled workers
- Neighbors

1. Ask how the project may have influenced them.
2. Ask if there is one particular area that they feel was most beneficial for them or their village.
3. Ask how DIVOG could improve on your methods.
4. Place each story/answer type into categories: Cat. 1, Cat. 2, Cat. 3, etc.
5. Arrange all of the stories/answers from all of the villages surveyed according to matching or similar answers. Tabulate the answers from most given to least given. This shows you what the greatest transformational impact was. It should help you see what has been successful and perhaps what has not been achieved. Make adjustments to the program to address the weak results.

By applying the hard work of impact evaluation, DIVOG gained a deeper appreciation for the work they were doing, because results were apparent. They also learned how to make adjustments for greater success. And importantly, they were able to validate the theory they operated by and the methods they used to achieve success. Greater funding followed.

Impact Investing

An article read, "Interest and activity in impact investing is booming. Since 2010, many of the major development agencies and development finance institutions have either launched their own calls for impact investing proposals or accelerated their direct investments into impact investment funds" (Dichter et al. 2013). The basic idea behind impact investing in the social sector is that it creates positive impact along with a financial return. The notion assumes "going for-profit is the only way to drive financial and operational discipline" (Starr 2012). The idea may seem radical to organizations that work for social and spiritual good, but impact investing "is defined not only by risk and financial return, but also by social and environmental impact" (Brandenburg 2012).

Some social impact entrepreneurs believe many non-profit causes produce limited impact because they don't apply the rigors of a good for-profit business plan. If the non-profit functions well enough to generate financial returns, they are positioned to attract more investors to their cause.

At the same time, donors—especially major foundations—are looking for a good business plan that will create impact. That is, their most common questions are going to be about vision, method, and ultimately impact. They know that impact in the social and faith sectors can be hard to measure, but they ask for a measurement plan, nevertheless.

Although social sector non-profit and faith-based ministries would likely not become profit-oriented—and lose their tax exempt status—the notion of impact investing in terms of financial returns to attract more investors is something they need to consider. That is, the principles behind impact investing—generating greater impact—can also attract more financial investors from the giving community.

When social and faith-based organizations do attempt to plan for impact, applying this process is spotty, depending on circumstances from project to project. That is because of the lack of dedication to this area. Naturally, much of their time is spent on doing the work. However, this is the problem. If non-profit agencies do not apply the rigor of creating more impact to attract more donor funds it could result in two things: 1) they won't learn how to improve processes, and 2) they won't attract more funding to expand their work.

Confidence and trust are at stake. Donors are losing confidence in the non-profit sector—what they believe are weak practices may reduce positive impact. Simple logic says for-profit development agencies are more likely to operate with greater discipline for greater results in the areas of planning, operating, and accounting. This concern over the lack of discipline for greater impact is creeping into the religious non-profit sector too.

With mission agencies, applying the process of impact planning has been spotty at best. For reaching the remaining groups who have not heard the gospel, impact planning and measurement methods will need to be highlighted in fundraising appeals.

This isn't to suggest that mission agencies give up their 501(c)(3) status and begin operating as for-profit businesses. But as more donors desire to see greater impact in their investment giving, mission agencies will need to operate with greater discipline to show they are indeed serious about impact.

To know how you are doing in this area, here are five questions you should ask:

1. Does our organization clearly understand the sort of impact we hope to achieve?
2. Do we work closely with our field partners to agree over what success will look like?
3. In working with our partners, have we designed a project that is culturally appropriate with clearly defined roles, goals, and expectations?
4. Have we developed a way to monitor how we are doing in achieving short-term and long-term impact goals?
5. Is there enough funding to ensure success, and is it calculated in ways to avoid wasting human and financial resources?

If the answers to questions 1–5 are "yes," then you are indeed operating like a for-profit business, but with all of the benefits and advantages that church and mission agencies enjoy from their non-profit status. This should attract more lasting donors to your cause.

Greater Results through Collective Impact

There are literally thousands of small social sector and faith-based non-profit organizations that work independently. Most have small annual budgets ($50,000 to $1 million), and they employee a small number of people. Most non-profits depend greatly on voluntary service. The organization may be working to alleviate a symptom, change a direction, intervene in a situation, or simply just be available as needed. However, the kinds of social or spiritual problems these organizations tackle are often complex. Small organizations don't have the people or money to tackle complex issues, so they just focus on the one thing they do. As a result, they create some positive impact in one area, but how much difference does it make, and is it lasting?

Food banks are a good example. They generally receive funds from local government programs and individual donations. Their mission is simple: gather food from businesses and homes and deposit it in a central location to help economically distressed people and communities. Their service is an intervention. People are hungry, and food banks provide food. Hunger is a symptom of a more complex problem. The fact that there are people who can't afford to buy enough food to feed their families is the problem. What caused these people to fall into this situation is a complex question. How to help them in the long term usually requires a more complex solution.

The word "complex" scares Christian ministries and social sector non-profits, which is one reason why they avoid addressing long-term solutions. They assume they must be the ones to focus on other needed activities to stamp out hunger. The courageous ones who do broaden their focus by adding more departments and more employers will probably see more success, if these things are done well. But now their agency has become more complex, and that requires more layers of administrative bureaucracy. The organization becomes less nimble. They spend more time maintaining the organization with less time to focus on the one area they are most passionate about.

Collective impact does not necessarily mean joining forces with other food banks so more food is collected and distributed. Rather, it is achieved when there is cross-sector collaboration. These days, donors, especially large foundations, desire greater impact, so they look for organizations and ministries that exhibit more cross-sector partnership.

For example, a church planting ministry works in a region where few churches exist. They train believers to strengthen the local church and to start new churches in other areas. But there are significant barriers to achieving greater success. The people they desire to help speak a language that has no written form. It is only a spoken language. They are also suspicious of religious material produced in a regional or national language, i.e., a domineering language. How far could the church planting ministry go in deepening people's understanding of Scripture if it is only accessible in a distrusted language? And even when there is material in the local language, most people in such isolated regions have low literacy rates. They are oral learners who pass on important information orally. These are significant barriers to greater success for the church planting ministry.

In the same way, a Bible translation agency can produce new translations, but if they don't produce training materials and multimedia distribution strategies, their success will be limited. If an organization that shows films as a way to introduce people to the Bible has no way to follow up with people who express interest, then impact diminishes as people stop thinking about the film they watched or the decision they made after viewing it.

This is where cross-sector collaboration can create collective impact for all of these organizations. Rather than any one of these sorts of agencies becoming more complex by branching out into discipleship training, linguistics, translation, film, and oral methods for learning, they form a collaborative partnership. Within the partnership, each one does what they do best, but they do it in a coordinated fashion. That means they operate with an agreed execution strategy, share resources, and account for outcomes and impact using the same processes. This way, each organization can achieve greater impact because other critical areas that contribute to their success are applied by agency partners.

Organizations that cling to their independent ways may find fewer donor dollars flowing their way as more donors look for collective impact as a criterion for funding.

7
THE WAY FORWARD: PRACTICAL ADVICE

The combination of money, good planning, and sacrificial service can be a powerful force for good when a partnership collaboration that brings these areas together is thriving. Building a thriving partnership requires humility, honesty, and mutual respect. It also requires patience and perseverance, because human nature in general and inequality in education, income, and living standards specifically can threaten partnership alliances from the start. Additionally, information gaps, which often lead to wrong assumptions, can deter the building of healthy partnerships. Historical church structures divided believers into hierarchical categories, and that has not helped the donor-recipient relationship either. Hopefully the church is moving beyond this and will now be valuing each individual as a co-minister in God's global mission. The following section offers advice for donors and recipients to bear in mind when forming a partnership alliance.

The Funding Proposal Process

TO THE RECIPIENT
The funding proposal process may seem cumbersome and time consuming. Even so, try to judge the process by the kind of information the donors are requesting. Do the questions inform you about important things you had not thought about? Do the questions sound naïve given your insider knowledge? Have you sought broad input from the people you serve for additional insights that you or the donor would benefit from knowing? A beneficial proposal process does take time, and the investment of time can help bridge understanding between the donor and the recipient. It builds

a common understanding of the challenges, risks, goals, and importantly, what success will look like. So in addition to the project design side, view the process also as a critical step in relationship building.

TO THE DONOR

Rather than a tersely worded form to collect information from a potential grantee, a funding proposal should be more of a dynamic and iterative design process. The form should ask the kinds of questions that help the potential recipients conceptualize how they will accomplish their visionary ideas. It should be more of a discovery process for the people making the proposal, and in the end they will view it as their design, instead of a series of answers just to get money. In addition, it is important to talk through the funding proposal with the people first to ensure they understand the process and especially the reasons behind the questions donors ask. The donor should also show flexibility in the process if their form is misaligned in places within the cultural context.

The Progress Reporting Process

TO THE RECIPIENT

Project reporting cycles seem to come around very fast, so reporting can feel burdensome to the people in charge of producing progress reports for donors. This is a reality for people more focused on the urgencies of day-to-day ministry work. Nevertheless, a good reporting process can function as a valuable internal self-monitoring tool for the ministry to know how they are doing in accomplishing their goals, and if not for donor reporting requirements, self-evaluation would probably occur less frequently, if at all. In addition, funding recipients should not view the report form as a watchdog questionnaire and take it as a sign of mistrust. Instead, they should be able to see it as an opportunity to raise the donor's awareness of the good things happening and the problems they are encountering. This is a way to build trust with donors who care about problems and obstacles to progress that crop up from time to time. Providing quality information on the good and the bad helps donors feel more like a partner instead of simply a source of money, or worse, a person to be appeased so their funding can continue. More likely, funding will continue with informative, honest, and regular reporting, especially if the report includes solutions to problems that crop up from time to time.

TO THE DONOR

Donors generally live in a world where information can be obtained quickly, so they sometimes forget that this is not the case in many of the places where ministry and mission projects exist. In one Southeast Asian country, gathering information on project progress was very time consuming because of the isolation of the workers, the political sensitivity of their work, and the lack of a communication infrastructure. In this situation, providing good quality donor reports just twice a year required a significant expenditure of time and money.

In addition, designing a progress report form requires careful thought. As mentioned above, a good report form doesn't just collect information on finances and anecdotes. It should also help funding recipients evaluate their own performance so they know how they are doing. Therefore, donors need to think beyond their own information context and develop reporting instruments that make sense to the recipients and are useful to them as well.

The Project Phase Review

TO THE DONOR AND THE RECIPIENT

With projects that have a distant finish line (five to ten years), it is difficult to predict how well they will progress until completion, because there are too many unknowns. Therefore, breaking a project into phases can be beneficial for many reasons. For example, dividing a nine-year project into three-year phases allows the partners to plan more vigorously for certain short-term benchmarks while keeping an eye on the long-term goals. This also makes a way for all partners to conduct an in-depth progress review every few years. While this may seem like an extra burden, a phase review allows the partners to slow down for the moment and take a fresh and hard look at how things are going. It is a regrouping time when each partner can evaluate how the collaboration is working. Importantly, a phase review usually identifies slowly building situations that will become a major threat to the project if not dealt with sooner. Whether hidden or simply neglected, unaddressed problems have a way of going beyond the point of no return. The issues become too difficult to overcome, so the partnership collapses. Pausing to occasionally make a fresh assessment of the state of affairs, on the part of all partners, is a proactive way to keep the partnership collaboration strong.

The Project Completion Stage

TO THE DONOR AND THE RECIPIENT

This stage is one of the most important times in the donor and funding recipient relationship, yet it is one of the most neglected stages. Much time and energy are spent developing a new partnership to ensure a smooth launch and good working relationship during the course of the collaboration; however, few people think about the importance of good closure.

In previous times, mission and ministry workers often assumed that donors would continue funding their work as long as progress was made, and indeed, many donors have shown amazing endurance in their giving. Even so, there is an increase in what some people refer to as "donor fatigue." Donor fatigue in giving is caused by numerous factors. Assuming a project is making steady progress, fatigue could set in because the donor feels disconnected from the results due to the recipient's infrequent outcome reporting. It could also be because the donor sees other pressing needs in the world that could benefit from their financial help. Another common reason for donor fatigue is simply the lack of feeling that something has been accomplished and is worthy of celebration. Everyone needs recognizable and recognized milestones.

A sense of accomplishment is the most rewarding part for many donors, so with projects that have a limited timeframe, project leaders need to make sure that some sort of clear closure is marked and celebrated with the donors. This is a good time to remind the donors about the long-term impact the project will have on the people and their community. Importantly, this is also the time when mission organization leaders thank the donors for their participation and then release them if the project has reached completion. Releasing them is a significant step of faith for any ministry, but it doesn't mean they cannot make another funding appeal to the donor for a new project or a new phase in an ongoing project. However, it does create a feeling of successful closure for donors who may want to move on without feeling like they are abandoning people. If the collaboration was successful and rewarding to the donor, then they may indeed commit funding for another project.

With ministry efforts that seek ongoing financial support for work that has no clear closure date, celebrating significant milestones is one way to help donors appreciate how their giving is making a difference in people's lives. Still, it is not realistic to assume most donors will remain engaged with a particular ministry effort for long, undefined periods, so finding ways to include new donors at particular significant junctures in the work is necessary. This means, once again, expressing a clear vision with meaningful outcomes and impact to a new potential funding partner.

Final Thoughts

The goal of this final section was to convey practical understanding of what true partnership collaboration in a social, ministerial, or missionary effort looks like. In regard to the donor and the funding recipient, it means that each person doesn't just think about what the other person can provide for them through the collaboration. Instead, they consider how their role can be carried out in such a way as to help the other be successful in what they are tasked to do.

With this model, the funding recipients understand the donor's high spiritual calling to be a wise investor of what God has entrusted to them, so they honor them by cooperating in ways that help them to be successful in their role. In the same way, donors understand the difficulties, disruptions, and threats many ministry workers must endure to be successful in their God-given roles, so they honor them by working hard to ensure that their financial role is helping and not hurting the workers and their cause. In the end, the people served by partnership collaboration benefit in rich ways. That is the ultimate goal of the collaboration, to create beneficial change with and for people living on the margins.

APPENDIX

Factors That Influence Giving

The following information is from a survey conducted by Metadigm Group for The Seed Company, Arlington, Texas.[28] The goal of the survey was to find out what influences high net-worth donors to give to mission and ministry projects in this age of global giving. The survey was conducted by a third-party organization that specializes in impact measurement metrics. Donor partners assume that their money, network/contacts, or experiences are needed when an organization invites them to a meeting.

- Donor partners are honored and interested in contributing time and expertise when there is a clear purpose and probability that the organization will be able to use the results to improve its rate of return and their capacity to help others invest.

- Those who have already participated in phone interviews or research indicate they are happy to do so and that it is beneficial to them and the organization.

- Donor partners indicate that they are drawn to give when a vision for ministry is clearly articulated, yet they also seek confirmation and the leading of the Holy Spirit when making a decision.

---

28 "Factors That Influence Giving." 2009. Unpublished report. The Seed Company and Metadigm Group. Used with permission from The Seed Company, Arlington, TX.

- Donor partners value organizations that help them to
  communicate their priorities of giving and their values
  for Christian ministry to their children and family
  members. Human interest stories about translation staff
  and the communities in which they work will engage
  whole families in the decision to give. Websites, print
  stories, and communications for younger family members
  were suggested. Prayer points, relating to the personnel
  and the project, along the translation project's progress
  are more desirable than impersonal progress reports.

- It would be good for donors to be able to visit a project or field
  in which a project is sponsored; some indicated that they would
  like to have their teen and older children accompany them.

- There is concern that effective plans and partnerships be in
  place to fully optimize the impact of a completed translation.

- Follow-up information on completed projects would be
  beneficial and help donor partners understand the long-
  term impact on culture and community of the projects they
  have funded.

- Precision and clarity of the vision and purpose for which the
  contribution will be used must be communicated well.

- Communication and definition of vision should be constantly
  reworked with input from significant donor partners.

- A clear plan with deliverables, timelines, operational
  milestones, and partnerships for long-term effectiveness are
  appreciated by business-savvy donor partners.

- Adequate resources have been secured to both initiate and
  substantially complete a project.

- Honest/transparent feedback demonstrating effective
  leadership, networking, and integrity is expected.

- High-end donor partners do not expect everything to go perfectly. They hope that communication on project health includes difficulties encountered, challenges, disappointments, and responses to these issues.

- The broader impact of the project and its applications to ancillary outcomes should be defined as comprehensively as possible. This is particularly important when communicating the potential impact of Scriptures rendered in mother-tongue languages and the resulting impact on literacy and community cohesion.

- Christian donor partners expect to sense the leading of the Holy Spirit and confirmation of the spiritual impact when a donation is made.

- Unlike business decisions, donor partners indicated that family members are often very involved in making decisions about ministry sponsorship.

- Donor partners are encouraged when organizations show initiative in attracting and developing new donors and donations to the ministry (e.g., gifts-in-kind).

- Personalized communication from a person (friend or development representative) with whom they have developed a relationship is highly prized. Impersonal or generalized communications are not highly motivational. Donor partners expect to hear/learn information that is new and relevant.

Developing a Memorandum of Understanding (MOU)

MOUs are commonly used in social and religious sector non-profit joint ventures. The idea is to produce a record of what all parties agree to do, for future reference if necessary. A simple MOU states these things in very brief and informal terms. A rigorous MOU reads more like a contract in case a disagreement arises later. This sort of MOU has greater implications and should be worked out with the help of experts.

Should a donor and his/her direct recipient produce an MOU? The combination of money, good planning, and sacrificial service can be a powerful force for good when a partnership collaboration that brings these areas together is thriving. Building a thriving partnership requires humility, honesty, and mutual respect. Additionally, information gaps, which often lead to wrong assumptions, can also deter the building of healthy partnerships.

For these reasons, it is a good idea for a donor and his or her recipient to document their roles, goals, and desired outcomes before they agree to collaborate. It is a way to protect the relationship for the benefit of the people both parties serve. Western agency MOUs tend to sound mistrusting, especially to small agency leaders in non-Western contexts, even though that is not the intent. Therefore, MOU wording should capture the trust relationship in a way that communicates mutual respect with cultural sensitivity.

Some things to include in a simple MOU between donor and recipient:
- Names of the people/agencies agreeing to work together.
- Beginning and end date of the partnership period.
- Final outcomes: state briefly through quantification and qualification what success will look like.
- Benchmarks: the key indicators of progress and the time when they should occur during the course of the project.
- Finances: how much money will be given by the donor, the frequency and the method of giving.
- Reporting: how the recipient will report on progress and how often.
- Exceptions, such as what the money should not be used for.
- Termination: agree to withdraw from the partnership at any time or commit to staying with the partnership for specific length of time.
- MOU templates abound. See http://moutemplates. com, for example. Not all of them are suitable for direct donor-recipient relationships, but they may provide ideas for other things to document in an MOU.

REFERENCES

Bhagat, Vinay, Pam Loeb, and Mark Rovner. 2010. "The Next Generation of American Giving." Blackbaud, Inc. (formerly Convio). http://www.convio.com/files/next-gen-whitepaper.pdf.

Bishop, Matthew, and Michael Green. 2008. *Philanthrocapitalism: How the Rich Can Save The World*. New York: Bloomsbury.

Brandenburg, Margot. 2012. "Impact Investing's Three Measurement Tools." *Stanford Social Innovation Review*. http://www.ssireview.org/blog/entry/impact_investings_three_measurement_tools.

Brooks, Arthur C. 2002. *Who Really Cares: The Surprising Truth about Compassionate Conservatism*. New York: Basic Books.

Corbett, Steve, and Brian Fikkert. 2009. *When Helping Hurts: How to Alleviate Poverty Without Hurting The Poor . . . and Yourself*. Chicago: Moody.

Davies, Rick, and Jess Dart. 2005. "The 'Most Significant Change' (MSC) Technique: A Guide to its Use." http://www.mande.co.uk/docs/MSCGuide.pdf.

Dichter, Sasha, Robert Katz, Harvey Koh, and Ashish Karamchandani. 2013. "Impact Investing: Closing the Pioneer Gap." *Stanford Social Innovation Review* 11 (1):36–43. http://www.ssireview.org/articles/entry/closing_the_pioneer_gap.

Douglas, Lois. 2006. "Globalizing Theology and Theological Education." In *Globalizing Theology*, edited by Craig Ott and Harold A. Netland. Grand Rapids: Baker.

Escobar, Samuel. 1991. "A Movement Divided: Three Approaches to World Evangelization Stand in Tension with One Another." *Transformation* 8(4):7–13.

———. 2003. *The New Global Mission: The Gospel from Everywhere to Everyone*. Downers Grove, IL: InterVarsity Press.

Godin, Seth. 2008. *Tribes, We Need You to Lead Us*. New York: Penguin.

Govindarajan, Vijay, and Chris Trimble. 2010. *The Other Side of Innovation: Solving the Execution Challenge*. Boston: Harvard Business Press.

Gravelle, Gilles. 2013. "Mission Reinvention: Why Some Leaders Think it is Urgent." Moving Missions. http://movingmissions.org/wp-content/pdfs/mission-reinvention.pdf.

Green, Stanley W. 2011. "Mission, Missionary, and Church Accountability That Counts: Implications of Integrity, Strategy, and Dynamic Continuity." In *Accountability in Missions: Korean and Western Case Studies*, edited by Jonathan J. Bonk, 71–82. Eugene, OR: Wipf & Stock.

Johnson, Todd M., and Kenneth R. Ross, eds. 2009. *The Atlas of Global Christianity*. Edinburgh: Edinburgh University Press.

Keller, Tim. 2002. "Why Plant Churches?" http://apostles-raleigh.org/wp-content/uploads/2012/08/Why_Plant_Churches-Keller.pdf.

Kotter, John P. 2012. *Leading Change*. Boston: Harvard Business Press. Kindle edition.

———. 1995. "Leading Change: Why Transformation Efforts Fail." *Harvard Business Review* (March–April): 60.

Lee, Shin Chul. 2011. "Accountability in Mission: A Case Study of Korea Presbyterian Mission." In *Accountability in Missions. Korean and Western Case Studies*, edited by Jonathan J. Bonk, 232–239. Eugene, OR: Wipf & Stock.

Lingenfelter, Sherwood G. 2008. *Leading Cross-Culturally: Covenant Relationships for Effective Christian Leadership*. Grand Rapids: Baker Academic.

Mansfield, Stephen. 2009. *The Search for God and Guinness: A Biography of the Beer that Changed the World*. Nashville: Thomas Nelson.

McLeish, Barry. 2007. *Yours, Mine & Ours: Creating a Compelling Donor Experience*. New Jersey: John Wily & Sons.

Missio Nexus. 2013. "Mission CEO Survey 2013: Navigating Global Currents." http://www.missionexus.org/2013-mission-ceo-survey/.

Moreau, A. Scott. 2008. "Short-term Missions in the Context of Missions, Inc." In *Effective Engagement in Short-term Missions: Doing it Right!*, edited by Robert J. Priest, 1–33. Pasadena: William Carey Library.

Morino, Mario. 2011. *Leap of Reason: Managing to Outcomes in an Era of Scarcity*. Washington, DC: Venture Philanthropy Partners. Kindle edition.

Neill, Stephen. 1964. *A History of Christian Missions*. London: Penguin.

Noll, Mark A. 1985. "Common Sense Traditions and American Evangelical Thought." *American Quarterly* 37 (2): 216–38.

Osili, Una, Reema Bhakta, Melissa Brown, Deborah Hirt, Cynthia Hyatte, Sindhu Raghavan, Xiaonan Kou, Jeffrey Small, and Shannon Neumeyer. 2010. "The 2010 Study on High Net Worth Philanthropy: Issues Driving Charitable Activities Among Affluent Households." The Center on Philanthropy at Indiana University. http://www.philanthropy.iupui.edu/files/research/2010baml_highnetworthphilanthropy.pdf.

Park, Paul. 2011. "Funders Aren't Investors, They're Purchasers." *Stanford Social Innovation Review*. http://www.ssireview.org/opinion/entry/funders_arent_investors_theyre_purchasers/.

Payne, J.D. 2012. *Strangers Next Door: Immigration, Migration and Mission*. Downer's Grove, IL: InterVarsity Press.

Peterson, Roger, Gordon Aeschliman, and R. Wayne Sneed. 2008. *Maximum Impact in Short-Term Mission*. Minneapolis: STEM Press.

Plueddemann James E. 2006. "Theological Implications of Globalizing Missions." In *Globalizing Theology: Belief and Practice in an Era of World Christianity*, edited by Craig Ott and Harold A. Netland, 256. Grand Rapids: Baker.

Priest, Robert J. 2006. "Researching the Short-Term Mission Movement." *Missiology: An International Review* 34 (4): 431–50.

————, ed. 2008. *Effective Engagement in Short-term Missions: Doing it Right*. Pasadena: William Carey Library.

Reese, Robert. 2010. *Roots & Remedies of the Dependency Syndrome in World Missions*. Pasadena: William Carey Library.

Rickett, Daniel. 2012a. "Part 1: Lean on Me: The Problem of Dependency," *Evangelical Missions Quarterly* 48 (1).

————. 2012b. "Part 2: Walk with Me: The Path to Interdependency" *Evangelical Missions Quarterly* 48 (2).

Rowell, John. 2006. *To Give or Not to Give: Rethinking Dependency, Restoring Generosity & Redefining Sustainability*. Georgia: Authentic.

Stanley, Brian. 1998. "The Legacy of Robert Arthington." Cambridge Center for Christianity Worldwide. Http://www.martynmission. cam.ac.uk/pages/centre/archive-seminar-papers/published-papers. php?searchresult=1&sstring=arthington.

Starr, Kevin. 2012. "Premature Incorporation: Don't Let It Happen to You." *Stanford Social Innovation Review*. http://www.ssireview. org/blog/entry/premature_incorporation.

Stern, Ken. 2013. *With Charity for All: Why Charities are Failing and a Better Way to Give*. New York: Double Day.

Stravers, Dave. 2012. *Measuring What Matters: Accountability and the Great Commission*. Mission India.

Stone, Chris. 2001. In *Effective Capacity Building in Non-Profit Organizations* prepared by McKinsey and Co., 45. Venture Philanthropy Partners. http://www.vppartners.org/sites/default/ files/reports/full_rpt.pdf.

Surowiecki, James. 2005. *The Wisdom of Crowds*. New York: Anchor Books.

Tanur, Judith M., ed. 1992. *Questions about Questions: Inquiries into the Cognitive Bases of Surveys*. New York: Russell Sage Foundation.

The Lausanne Movement. 2007. "The Lausanne Standards: Giving and Receiving Money in Mission." http://www.lausanne.org/en/ documents/lausanne-standards.html.

Vallet, Ronald E. and Charles E. Zech. 1995. *The Mainline Church's Funding Crisis: Issues and Possibilities*. Grand Rapids: Wm. B. Eerdmans.

Ver Beck, Kurt Alan. 2008. "Lessons from the Sapling: Review of Quantitative Research in Short-term Missions." In *Effective Engagement in Short-term Missions: Doing it Right*. edited by Robert J. Priest, 475–502. Pasadena: William Carey Library.

Walls, Andrew F. 1990. "The American Dimension in the History of the Missionary Movement." In *Earthen Vessels: American Evangelicals and Foreign Missions, 1880–1980*, edited by Joel A. Carpenter and Wilbert R. Shenk, 13. Grand Rapids: Wm B. Eerdmans.

———. 2005. *The Cross-Cultural Process in Christian History: Studies in the Transmission and Appropriation of Faith*. Maryknoll, NY: Orbis Books.

———. 1988. "Missionary Societies and the Fortunate Subversion of the Church." *Evangelical Quarterly* 60: 141–155.

Wei-Skillern, Jane C., James E. Austin, Herman B. Leonard, Howard H. Stevenson. 2007. *Entrepreneurship in the Social Sector*. London: Sage.

Willard, Dallas. 1988. *The Spirit of the Disciplines: Understanding How God Changes Lives*. San Francisco: HarperCollins.

Willmer, Wesley K., ed. 2008. *A Revolution in Generosity: Transforming Stewards to be Rich Toward God*. Chicago: Moody.

Winter, Ralph. 1992. "A Response to 'A Movement Divided.'" *Transformation* 9 (1): 26.

Yung, Hwa. 2004. "Strategic Issues in Missions—An Asian Perspective." *Evangelical Missions Quarterly* 40 (1): 26–34.

Zimmerman, Brenda. 2013. "Embracing Complexity, Connectivity, and Change." Lecture at Next Generation Evaluation Conference (November 14). Stanford University. *Stanford Social Innovation Review*. http://www.ssireview.org/nextgenevaluation.